P9-CRU-766

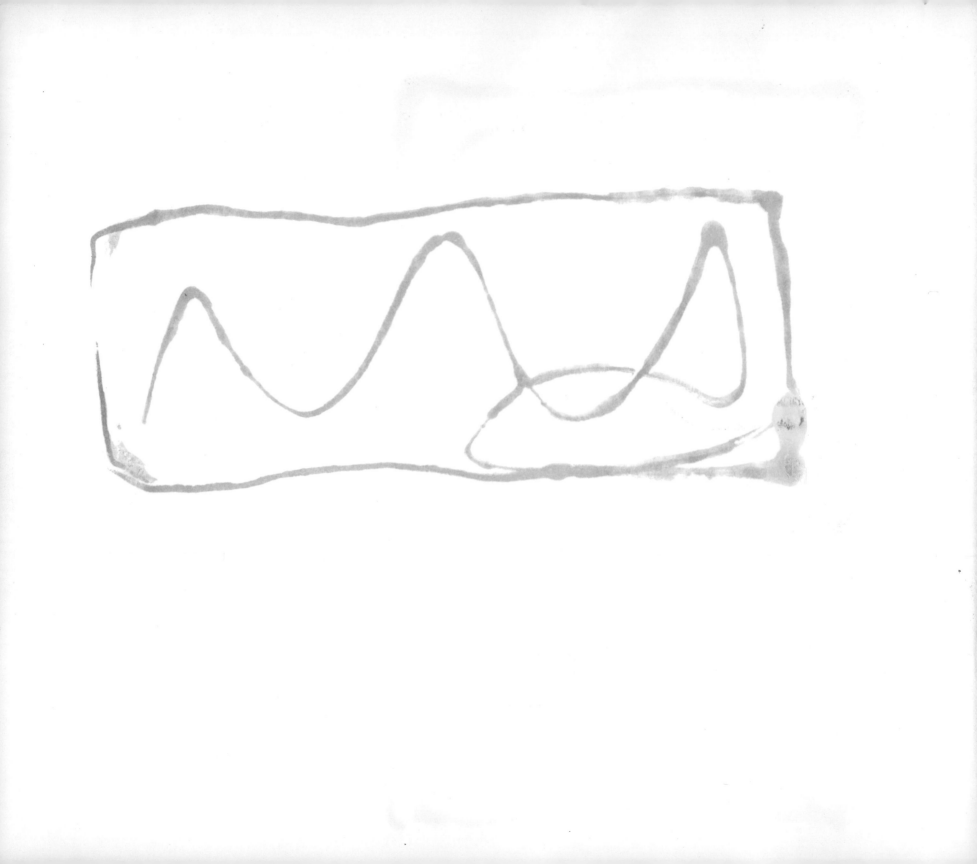

TRANSWHICHICS

TRANSWHICHICS

DUFOUR EDITIONS

POETRY BY ERNEST M. ROBSON

9/1975
Am. Lit

PS
3568
O318
T7

ACKNOWLEDGEMENT

The authors are quite grateful for assistance in the experimental development of prosodyne cues to:

Dr. John W. Black, Director of Speech Research, The Ohio State University.

Dr. Samuel Litwin, Statistician, Professor in the Operational Research Division of the Penn Wharton School of the Univ. of Pennsylvania.

Dr. Stanley K. Smith, Chairman, Department of Psychology, Albright College, Reading, Pennsylvania.

The authors wish to thank Betty Adams for her editorial assistance.

Marion Robson lettered Prosodynic Script and contributed to all phases of research that developed this book. Book design and illustration by James Lowell Adams. Copyright—Ernest and Marion Robson 1969.

Library of Congress Number 74-121306

ISBN — (Cloth) 0 8023 1249 7 — (Paper) 0 8023 1250 0

Printed by Smale's Printery, Pottstown, Pa. 19464

Published by Dufour Editions Inc., Chester Springs, Pa. 19425

Contents

Introduction

It is the philosophy which underlies its techniques that lends significance to this book. The philosophy is historical and cultural. It guided the selection of themes and the construction of images throughout the poems in this volume; and, in many ways, it molded the careers and life of the author.

The cultural concept of this book is, simply, that culture is the way we imagine existence.

This concept includes our image of ourselves, our image of others, and the way we look at the physical world around us. The ways we see and imagine our physical surroundings depend on whether we are confronted with the wilderness of the night sky, the seas, and uninhabited terrains or artificial, man-made environments of cities, parks, farms, cultivated fields, transportation structured areas. The understanding and richness of our outlook towards the man-made sectors of our physical world depend on our knowledge and feel for the technology that produced them. These, in turn, depend on our grasp of the scientific and engineering relationships which determine and pervade our technology. Furthermore, our perceptions and concepts of the "wilderness" sectors of our surroundings are made and coloured and shaped by our technological orientation, our feeling and grasp for technology.

Always, with change two orientations interact: our mode of existence and our manner of imagining it. We anticipate change. What we don't expect to find is the rate of change that has characterized the 20th century. 20th century man has been confronted with a revolution in his means of production, transportation, and communication, that in terms of new energy levels has been more world-wide than any previous change of our recorded history. Yet the ideologies, the inter and infra human emotions, feelings, and expectancies; the forms of educational institutions; the organizations of cities and state populations; the attitudes of economic corporations and unions; the dreams, interests, and disciplines of the arts have not come to terms with this technological revolution. They have lagged way behind. The subjective world of man has lacked leadership that could make sense out of our mode of existence and give meaning to it. The most eloquent concept of the universe that the chief astronaut can send to Earth from his orbit of the moon is a quotation from the book of Genesis—an anachronistic piece of cosmology from which scientists could not be liberated without being burned at the stake; a complete denial of the orientation which put the astronauts into lunar orbit.

The field of poetry is a tiny area within the total subjective world. Still poems continue to be written and to appeal to different sized populations in all literate nations. When we ask: how many people reflect our technological revolution our question is not a trivial one. It is another form of the basic problem of our time: how to live with our technology in terms of a new cultural orientation. It is in this sense that this book is a philosophical experiment with poetry as test material.

Let us simplify these problems by asking two questions. How may a technologically sophisticated, science orientated society express its

attitudes towards "Nature" through a subjective art such as poetry? Secondly, under what conditions may poetry operate as an experimental art?

For workers in all the art fields there are different lenses, keys, and open sesames to vistas of "Nature" through the fine-grained information of the physical sciences. The poet may observe the extremely large or small events of Nature through instruments of science which reveal occurrences that otherwise would never be seen. Such instruments are: telescopes, microscopes and more complicated signal receivers such as machinery for acoustic spectographs, radio telescopes, and spectroscopes for all ranges of the electromagnetic wave. The images of stars, bacteria, structures of the voice, may be independently perceived in any number of ways by the poet, ways that detach the observation from its instrumental environment and connect it with existence and yield it as raw material for subjective interpretation. Several of the poems in this volume depend on observations through telescopes seen through the author's experience as an amateur astronomer.

Another way for scientific technology to influence an artist's view point towards "Nature" also depends on separating the information of science from the artificial environments of its experiments. Here we deal with the mythlike characterizations of our physical universe expressed by some scientific "laws" and equations. Examples are: the four energy "laws" of physics, the principle of least action, Einstein's $E=MC^2$, characterizations of chemical equilibria such as LeChatelier's

principle, information theories of symbol communication systems, etc. The activities in "Nature" expressed by these "laws" may influence poetry and art by selection of images and choice of themes. There are several poems in this book which have had their style affected by the mythlike characterizations of "Nature" by science.

One of the indisputable examples of the radical influence of "natural laws" on our way of life is the effect of changes in energy levels. Some illustrations of simple effects of shifts in energy levels are: change of color with temperature of materials; change of overtone structure with amplitude as well as our perceptions of shifts in pitch with change in loudness levels; differences in activity levels of the same person or species in temperate versus tropical zones on earth. The author learned in several experiments that variations in the acoustic energy levels of blocks of syllables and words in a poem tend to be associated with different subjective states and moods.

The kind of information discussed contributes to the imagination the same sort of content that the Greek pantheon gave to the ancient Mediterranean writers and artists and is similar in character to the mythlike cosmologies of the great religions. But there is a profound difference. The "Nature" ideas of the pre-scientific cultures were based on direct sensory observations of physical happenings; our most general "laws" of physics and chemistry are products of artificial operations of experiments, their man-made constructions and their mathematical language. Their ideas are far more implicit in their artificial environments than "hypotheses" suggest. Consequently, two blind alleys await the artist who wishes to orientate towards "Nature" via hypotheses of exact science.

First: hypotheses change. They are the tentative ideas of the scientific community, the intended targets of more exact measurements and contradictory discoveries. They should be considered a contribution of quicksand and poison for a poet's concepts of "Nature."

Secondly: the models of the exact sciences are mechanical because they operate only when recurrent events permit predictability. If the events were not recurrent they would not be predictable; and if they were not predictable there would be *no scientific proof*. Yet our existence is crowded with unorganized events in vague trends that show unexpected occurrences bordering or randomness. When will the next large meteorite fall on earth or the next virus mutation occur? Where will the next nova appear? Countless happenings in the physical universe are not predictable; in the human domain even less so. Now the poet's or artist's themes embrace all of an individual's or a society's existence. Totality of existence is the matrix of the creative artist. Clearly then, from the poet's view point the "laws" of science are unique characterizations of *limited fields*. They do not explain all of existence. Consequently, the mythlike generalizations of chemistry-physics, astrophysics, and bio-chemistry can contribute to a poet's concept of "Nature" as a pantheon of generic properties and qualities but never as features that are universal and irrevocably unchangeable. This does not mean that limitations of the "laws" of science make them trivial to the artist. This conclusion would be entirely erroneous. These abstract structures may influence themes of the composer; they will shape perspectives on "Nature"; and they will inevitably revolutionize the information potential of the art medium. Our culture is so dependent on and determined by its technology that no serious advances in any subjective field are likely to occur without coming to terms with our scientific technology. Without a background of scientific understanding no contemporary artist is likely to achieve the universality associated with great art. Humanists won't accept this statement. Yet that is the point of this book.

We face the second question: under what conditions may poetry operate as an experimental art?

The conditions that determine the validity of an objective scientific experiment are not the same for experimentation in a subjective work of art such as a poem. The former depend on repeatable procedures with predictable results; the latter on the rare occurrence, the inimitable process with its unforeseen conclusions. The criteria of excellence in subjectivistic experimentation are non-objective states of being as: sensory pleasure, imagination, excitement, stimulation of feeling, emotional satisfaction, depth and breath of vitality, intensity of interest.

There are unanalyzed acts of improvisation and spontaneity in the composition of most poems, paintings, and musical compositions. These spontaneities frequently are empathetic for audiences or specta-

tors. They usually speak with and in and through the style of the composition. Consequently, their effects are integral with the work of art itself. This subjective process is irrelevant to the deliberate quantitative analysis which a scientist utilizes in structuring a design for an experiment. The element of control is mandatory. Nor is this surprising when we consider a scientific experiment as a socialization of knowledge according to which any qualified worker who obeys the instructions of an experiment should end up with the same quantitative results as every other worker . . . within the permissible limits for error. Instructed operational controls are incompatible with the spontaneity of the creative artist. This does not exclude deliberate, conscious, and analytic techniques by many creative artists. Yet, in the most rationalized of works such as Poe's poems, Dante's masterpiece, Picasso's and Cezanne's experiments, Seurat's scientific paintings, the signature of a person with unique subjective associations pervades the composition. The artist, too, like the scientist is governed by disciplines without which nothing is accomplished. But the artist's game is a different game with subjective goals alien to the objective sciences and incompatible with rules for socializing discovery.

When a poem or painting or any other aesthetic expression is presented as "experimental" what then did the composer do or what are the characteristics of his composition that justifies our calling it "experimental"? Every effort to create a new poem or new painting is considered an experiment by the artist. But we require something more objective

than a composer's uncertainty about the outcome of a specific undertaking to consider it an authentic experiment.

There are two quite general ways for specifying an "experimental" art composition:

(1) The problem that the composer attempted to solve had never before been attacked. This is the criterion of "originality." Whether an artist is able or not to formulate clearly his "new" problem is quite irrelevant. Others will do this formulation later on. Actually, artists, poets, and composers are always quite interested in something new going on in their fields. It was an artist who bought the first Van Gogh. A poet, Baudelaire, was the first to fully appreciate the originality of Edgar Allen Poe. Then the news spread through the western world.

(2) An experiment occurs when a composer succeeds in solving a problem that is well known but still unsolved, or in carrying out the solution of a problem in finer and more perfect detail. The use of English blank verse was first developed by the poet Marlowe as a technique for introducing more natural speech into the theatre. After Marlowe's death blank verse was developed by Shakespeare into the highest level of linguistic art that has ever been written for dramatic performance.

These general criteria can be made more specific by asking three questions about alleged "experimental" compositions:

(1) were areas of existence never before handled by an artist introduced into a theme?

(2) did a poet or an artist increase the information capacity of the physical medium of his art?

(3) the third question is one of form. Does an ordering of art symbols fit a theme or evoke a subjective state with a fitness never before achieved?

According to these criteria there are many poems in this book that may justify themselves as "experiments." Physical features of the sounds of English have been analyzed, selected, and organized into written populations of words with redundancies designed to evoke new speech music, new associations with physical science, and, to introduce a broader and more diversified acoustic palette into poetry.

The sounds of English have been divided into two categories: acoustic characteristics of phonemes and "surprasegmentals." First we deal with phonemes. Phonemes categorize sounds. They designate the number of sounds in a language which can be auditorially discriminated by a native speaker in all contexts of representative speech and that may be written independently of one another. Phonemes may also be discriminated from one another by their capacity to change the meanings of words when one phoneme is substituted for another, i.e., a *cat* vs. a *cot* vs. a *cut* or a *sun* vs. a *pun* vs. a *nun*.

The phonemes of English, the fixed sounds of the language, that linguists categorize as "segmentals," were analyzed into their *acoustic dimensions* and their *acoustic qualities*. These may be classified as "sub-phonemic" traits. The acoustic dimensions of phonemes are: relative duration; their levels of amplitude or power; the frequency levels of vowel overtones or "formants." The latter may be considered as whispered pitch levels. Some acoustic qualities of phonemes, their identifiable traits are:

plosiveness, or sudden release or breath pressure, the "explosive" consonants [p] [tf] [k] [t]

nasality, the nasal humming sounds with their unpleasant association of whining [m] [n] [d]

fricativeness, the teeth or lip frictioned turbulance of the breath stream in our hissing sounds [f] [v] [s] [z] [o]

the open-mouthed breathy sounds, [w] [wh] [h] [j]

the bony-roof-sounding versus the soft-tongued phonemes, etc.

It is clear that these sub-phonemic traits reflect the *ways of speaking* the phonemes, the *timbre of materials* in our speech mechanism, and the three *measurable dimensions of the acoustic waves of speech:* time, power, frequency. The interest was: *what themes or things or events can sets of these components of English sounds best describe and subjectivize?* Description is the semantic problem; subjectivization is the problem of what taste and feelings can different phonetic patterns generate? The semantic equation is one of selecting words with meanings that fit and enhance subjective associations carried by the phonetic

pattern. There is nothing new about selecting words for both *the meaning of the words* and *the fit of their phonemes* into a pattern. This is what poets have done through the ages and still do when they select a word for its rime value as well as its meaning. Here the experiment was to utilize finer grained features of phonemes as: diphthong beats; blocks of slow and fast vowels; contours of low versus high whisper-pitched words; intrinsic power curves of syllables with varying inherent amplitudes, time durations and formant levels. A "formant" is the linguist's term for a characteristically resonated frequency region in the spectrum of a vowel. Other sub-phonemic patterns utilized the fuzzy timbres of fricatives, the whiny nasals, the soft impressions of lip sounds, etc. It was discovered that only by frequently repeating a trait-bearing vowel could a composition be rendered audible. The most audible and interesting phonetic patterns were the multidimensional ones where a few selected vowels were repetitively combined with a set of consonantal traits and timbres. Examples are discussed in notes on the poems. These phonetic constructions were in many compositions "firsts" and, accordingly, they qualify as genuine experiments to increase the information capacity of the physical medium of poetry. The constrictions of these phoneme techniques are similar to the restraints imposed by rimes i.e. words are selected *both* for *meaning* and *the fit of their vowels and consonants into an acoustic pattern.* The pattern, too, is a constraint. It is selected from many patterns for its ability to express the subjective theme of the poem and

to refer, objectively, to existence (things, events, etc.). When we look more closely at the differences in constraint caused by the acoustic techniques in these compositions and those imposed on the writer by rime it becomes evident that rime is far more restrictive. This subject calls for quantitative study of "degrees of freedom in poetry."

2. We have dealt with segmental acoustic patterns. We now for the first time introduce suprasegmental acoustic patterns into poetry. "Suprasegmental" forms are patterns of duration, loudness, fundamental pitch and pauses. Ordinary printed English does not present this information. Consequently, a set of graphic cues called "prosodynes" for "suprasegmental phonation" have been developed to cue the reader to speak as instructed on different levels of pitch and loudness, with different durations of speech, and periods of pauses. The suphonic code is presented in the appendix. Although many efforts have been made by many men over several centuries to incorporate the suprasegmentals into English script this is the first time that a set of these cues has been written into the orthography of English poems. That is why some compositions in this book are truly experiments to increase the information at the disposal of the poet, i.e. what he may choose to write.

The significance of suprasegmental information for poetry has been observed as a set of new potentials for the art. They are:

1. choices of transforming low to high information words and the reverse;

2. capacity to write cues for continuity between lines in a poem; cues with semantic carry-overs;

3. opportunities to enhance (for the reader) intrinsic acoustic patterns;

4. power to bring acoustic variety into refrains;

5. a potential for using orthographic contours to suggest the shape of feelings or things;

6. a technique for rendering the accent patterns of unknown, coined, or nonsense words more reliable for the reader who speaks the poem.

In due time other poets are likely to develop additional uses for written suprasegmental cues.

Because the language medium is about 50% redundant and operates with five key components: segments, suprasegments, grammar, word designations of existence (the most informative), and the syllable semantics (er, ed, ing, etc.), it is extremely difficult to quantify the information load of any one of the five components. This difficulty is compounded by the role of context, a synergistic role. In spite of this difficulty it seems to the author that suphonic script permits a poet to say things he could not say in conventional print; and, sometimes, to say much more in a few words than with many words in standard print.

The other experimental efforts have been thematic and were discussed under the question of attitudes towards Nature in a technically sophisticated society.

Urn drawn and computer randomized words have appeared in some poems. Randomized techniques are by no means "new" to poetry nor do these techniques make an "experiment." It is possible that the insistence on integrating random-generated words with the theme of these poems and with expressions of subjective states for the sake of continuity is a development of this approach. The author does not know whether these efforts deserve the honorific title of "experimental."

There has been confusion about the role of randomness in art because "noise" has not been clearly distinguished from the "uncertainty" due to an unrecognizably large number of choices. This is one error the author hopes he has not committed.

Conditions for judging an experiment in the subjective universe of the arts have been analyzed without concern for the question: what makes a poem or a painting be good or bad art? Now—no serious composer, willingly or knowingly, is likely to publish a bad composition or one he considers a failure. This question of good or bad poetry is involved with the problem of aesthetics or beauty, a problem with countless answers. I tend to agree with Poe's interpretation of "Beauty" as a function of taste and with Pablo Picasso's words: "I hate that aesthetic game of the eye and the mind played by these

connoisseurs, these Mandarins who "appreciate" beauty. What IS beauty, anyway? There's no such thing. I never appreciate any more than I like. I love or I hate . . . . . . etc.

Sometimes the question of beauty is mixed up with the question of significance. According to the philosophy of culture behind this book a work of art is significant when it makes the way we imagine existence more recognizable.

Beyond the problem of creating a poetry that harmonizes with our scientific orientation lies a deeper question. In what ways may our new technology yield information that can give universal meaning to our man-made worlds? Today . . . everywhere . . . this is the question the brighter students are asking. The answers lie outside the domain of poetry though they surely would project the most vital themes for poetry.

The question of the meaning of our lives can be broken up into two inquiries:

1. why were we born? This is the question of human destiny.

2. how may exploitation of man by man and animals by man be reduced and its pain mitigated? This is the fundamental question behind all reform: ideals, moralities, all heavens, utopias, and Hypoborean dreams.

All the great religions and philosophies, including Marxism, have been attempts to answer one or both of these questions. The position taken here—as in the case of poetry—is that only in union with our modern technology can these questions be answered for contemporaneous man.

A critique of cues for readers and speakers

The reader will notice that different poems are written in different print. Some compositions appear only in prosodynic print; other poems are presented in prosodynic orthography but are preceded by a version in standard English print. A third presentation is cued with prosodynes only here and there in short passages. A fourth group appears only in standard English print. These are the compositions that need no intensity, pause, pitch or time durational instruction because their phonetic patterns are cue-rich enough in acoustic dimensions for any native speaker of American English to hear the message in the standard print. The loud diphthong music in "The Voice of the Buoys," and the multi-dimensional phoneme music in "Lyric For a Flute" need no additional acoustic cues.

When a poem first appears in standard typography and then is presented in prosodynic print the double exposure is intended to give the reader an extra bit of information: the author's vocal intention, his ideal performance. The reader-speaker may then decide to accept or reject the author's model, but at least he knows the writer's intent in terms of what rendition the author prefers. Two script presentations are usually those poems whose images are associated with infrequent Occurrences such as astronomic images in "Transwhichics #1 and #2." Another criterion for double presentation is a poem with rhythm that violates the stress patterns of English for aesthetic-semantic reasons peculiar to the authors compositional design. Other grammatic cue determinants being absent, verbs in English are far more likely to be stressed than prepositions. Students trained in prosodynes marked "woodwinds" quite differently from the cued version of the refrain **BLEW**═N **FLEW**═N . Yet this is the formant music pattern the poet wrote into his theme. Another justification for a double typographic presentation is the need to acoustically sharpen the rhetorical style of a poem in order to transmit its theme with a finer flare. This purpose led to a dual script for "Stony River," "Pathways of the Suns," "Crows" and several other compositions.

The case of a partially cued script is "The Dirge of the Cold" where the low vowel diphthong music is sufficiently powerful to transmit its acoustic theme without additional cues. The animal cries throughout the poem are essential to the message of the theme; yet they are infrequent occurrences for urban readers. To compensate for the unfamiliarity of these happenings to so many potential readers, these passages were cast in cued script. It may interest some readers to know that even though the longer fluctuations of the loon's call does show in the print, the perturbations of the loon cry cannot be written with prosodynes. The duration of perturbations transpires in thousandths (milli) seconds which are too rapid for human speech to reproduce. It is a cardinal principle of this code not to instruct readers to speak the impossible. Consequently, only the valuable information of the longer waves appear in the script.

Where the theme of the poem depended more on suprasegmentals of speech than on any other set of cues no standard typography appears. Only the prosodynic script that carries the crucial information is presented. It is interesting to examine the linguistic conditions that render suprasegmental cues most informative. In "Hymn to a Rat Race" the sparse context of its pronouns and auxiliary verbs deprives these functional words of their identificational power and makes them quite meaningless. Their generality in non-contextual English must be cue-reinforced for the poem's theme to make any sense whatsoever. Therefor the poem is printed only in suprasegmentally cued script. Another instance of thematic dependency on suprasegmental speech is in "Soliloquy" where "phemes" such as (huh), (oo), (aw), (oh) acquire an attitudinal expression with and only with prosodynic script. Another poem to be enriched and written more reliably for the reader is "Voices in the Violins." The soft quiet middle section and the concentration of rapid and high pitched speech in the terminal passage could not be written without graphic cues.

These analyses show that considerable thought is required to justify the use of an independent set of cues in a cue-rich, 50% redundant, language such as English. The overlaps of multiple sets of cues at one moment give instructions to readers about the use of the language and the next moment tell the speakers to act in certain ways in the world outside of language and, continuously, operate as symbols that identify the recurrent events of human existence . . . these overlaps convert the problem of assessing the information load of any single set of cues into a question that is complicated and is more a matter of judgment than simplistic logic. For clarity we may summarize the criteria for writing more or less artificial cues into these poems. When English poetry *needs* acoustic messages to compensate for lack of context, then prosodynic cues are justified . . . otherwise they are superfluous. But isn't the justification of an art the creation of NEW CONTEXT? . . . out of its physical medium.

Cues for vowel pitch modulation

SAME VOWEL SPOKEN WITH RISING OR FALLING PITCH IN PERIODS CONTROLLABLE BY SPEAKER

NORMAL SPEED		SLOW SPEED	
RISE	FALL	RISE	FALL

SEE HER DO THE LOOP DE LOOP SHE'S A

FIRE BALL WHAT A SHOW DO YOU WANT

A BALLOON YEAHHH

ITS INCREDIBLE I NEVER THOUGHT HED EVEN

MAKE IT TO **FIRST** BASE YET THERE

HE IS LEADING THE PACK..........WHAT CAME OVER HIM

WAS IT HORSE SHOES THEY SAY ITS BETTER TO BE LUCKY

THAN GOOD

THERES NO RETURN.......THAT CANT

BE HE WENT LIKE THAT IT WAS JUST YESTERDAY

I SAW HIM

Prosodynes
DURATION

Trace	A E I O U THE of
Short	A E O I U W Y
Normal	A E I O U W Y
Prolonged	A E I O U Y

INTENSITY

Whisper level	a e i o u w y
Quiet unaccented speech (first amplitude level)	A E I O U W Y
Normal conversational effort (second amplitude level)	A E I O U W Y
Maximum stress or intensity (third amplitude level)	A E I O U W Y

Prosodynes (continued)

PITCH

Lowest pitch – indicated by depressing the vowels	M$_I$M M$_O$M M$_{AW}$M M$_{EE}$M
Middle pitch – indicated by normal position on line	MIM MOM MAWM MEEM
Highest pitch – indicated by elevating the vowels	M^{I}M M^{O}M M^{AW}M M^{EE}M

PAUSES

Intra-phrase pause, articulatory: blank space 2 times height of tallest letter.

Inter-phrase, for breath and syntax: blank space 4 times height of tallest letter.

Pause of thought: line of dots varying from 1 cm. to 3 cm. with time for decision.

Pause allocations require some semantic judgment by the writer.

TRANSWHICHICS

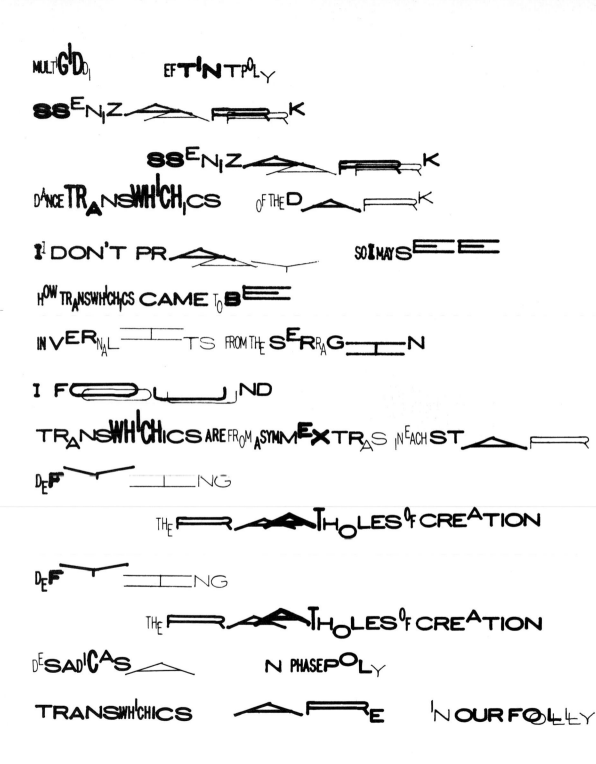

Multigidi   eftintpoly
Ssenizark
        Ssenizark
Dance transwhichics of the dark.

I don't pray, so I may see
How transwhichics came to be
In vernalits from the serragin.

I found
Transwhichics are from asymextras in each
    star
Defying
        The rat holes of creation.

Defying
        The rat holes of creation
Desadicasa N phasepoly
Transwhichics are in our folly.

TRANSWHICHICS 2

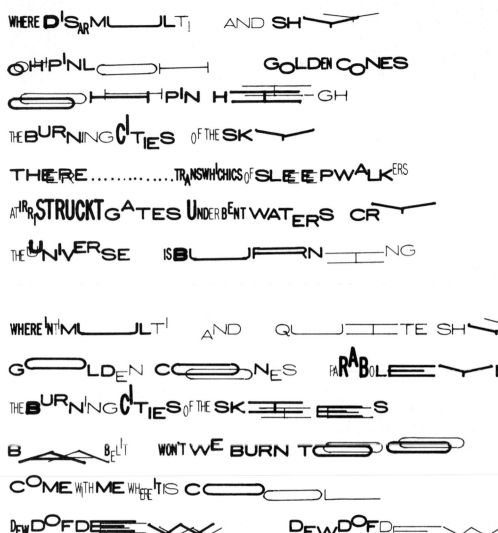

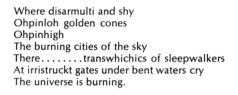

Where disarmulti and shy
Ohpinloh golden cones
Ohpinhigh
The burning cities of the sky
There........transwhichics of sleepwalkers
At irristruckt gates under bent waters cry
The universe is burning.

Where intimulti and quite shy
Golden cones paraboleyes
The burning cities of the skies
Babelit won't we burn too?
Come with me where it is cool
Dewdofdew   dewdofdew
Come with me where it is cool
Dewdofdew   dewdofdew.

PATHWAYS OF THE SUN

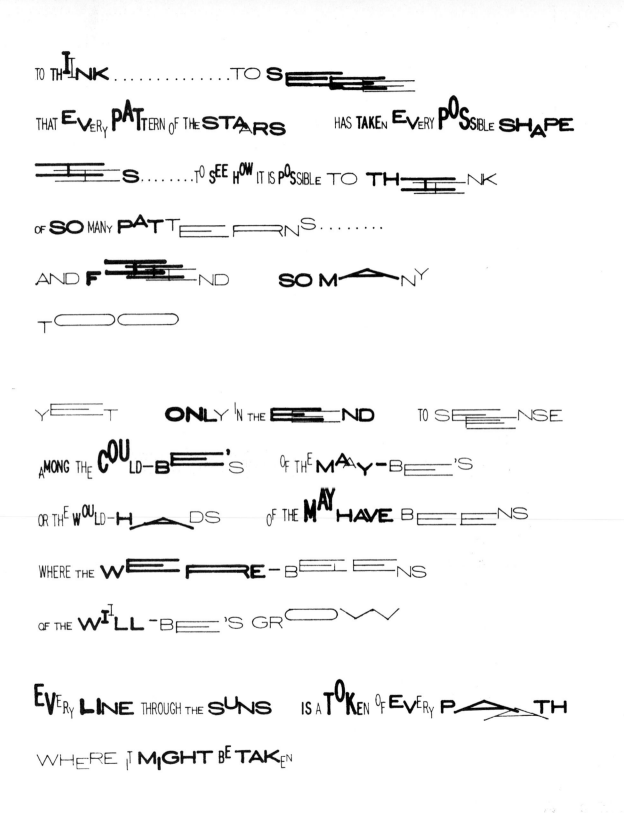

To think...............to see
That every pattern of the stars has taken every
    possible shape
Is....to see how it is possible to think of so
    many patterns....
And find so many
Too.

Yet...only in the end to sense
Among the could-be's of the may-be's
Or the would-hads of the may have-beens
Where the were-beens
Of the will-be's grow
Every line through the suns is a token of every
    path
Where it might be taken

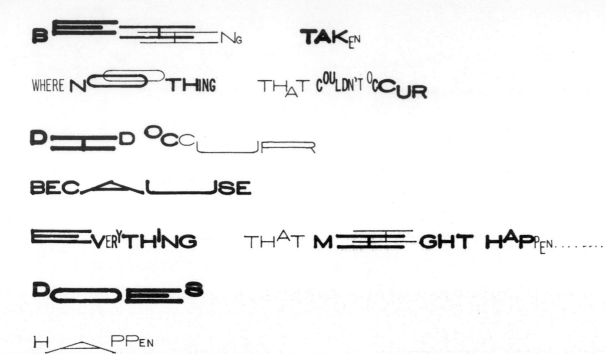

BEING TAKEN

WHERE NOTHING THAT COULDN'T OCCUR

DID OCCUR

BECAUSE

EVERYTHING THAT MIGHT HAPPEN.......

DOES

HAPPEN

Being....taken,
Where nothing that couldn't occur
Did occur
Because
Everything that might happen...
Does happen

TOWARDS LYRA AND THE SWAN

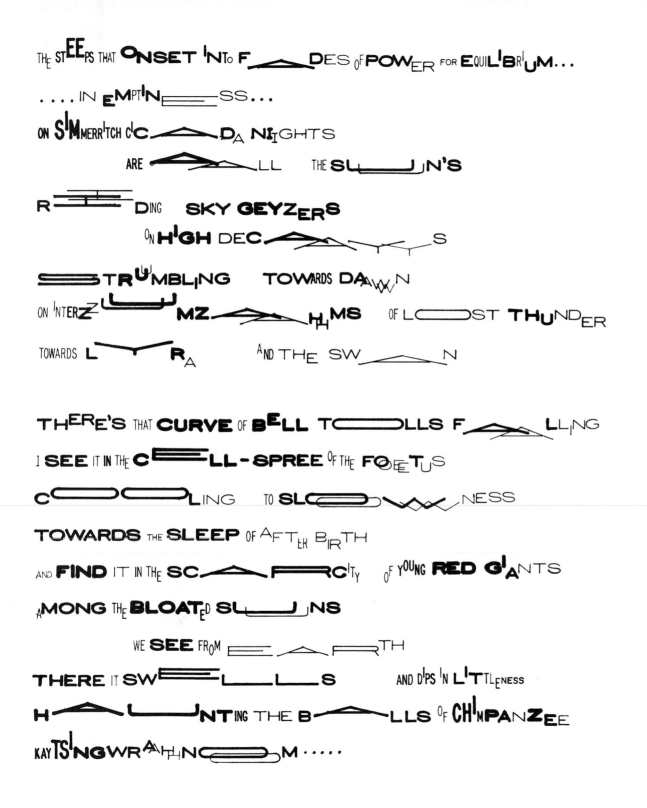

THE STEEPS THAT ONSET INTO F^DES OF POWER FOR EQUILIBRIUM...

....IN EMPTINESS...

ON SIMMERITCH CICADA NIGHTS

ARE ALL THE SUUN'S

R^DING SKY GEYZERS

ON HIGH DECAYS

STRUMBLING TOWARDS DAWWN

ON INTERZUMZ HUMS OF LOOST THUNDER

TOWARDS LYRA AND THE SWAN

THERE'S THAT CURVE OF BELL TOOLLS FALLING

I SEE IT IN THE CEELL-SPREE OF THE FOEETUS

COOLING TO SLOWNESS

TOWARDS THE SLEEP OF AFTER BIRTH

AND FIND IT IN THE SCARCITY OF YOUNG RED GIANTS

AMONG THE BLOATED SUUNS

WE SEE FROM EARTH

THERE IT SWEELLLS AND DIPS IN LITTLENESS

HAUNTING THE BALLS OF CHIMPANZEE

KAYTSINGWRAHHNOM.....

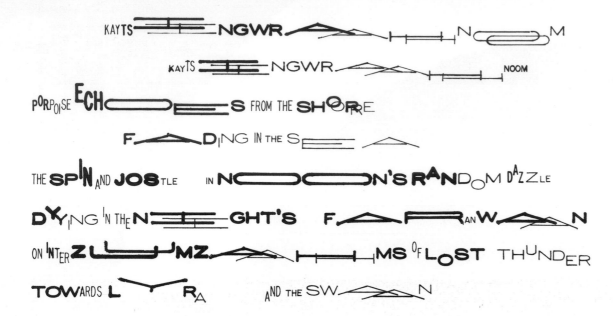

KAYTS ⸺ NGWR ⸺ N ⸺ M

KAYTS ⸺ NGWR ⸺ NOOM

PORPOISE ECHOES FROM THE SHORE

FADING IN THE SEA

THE SPIN AND JOSTLE IN NOON'S RANDOM DAZZLE

DYING IN THE NIGHT'S FAR RAN W AN

ON INTERZLUMZ ⸺ MS OF LOST THUNDER

TOWARDS LYRA AND THE SWAN

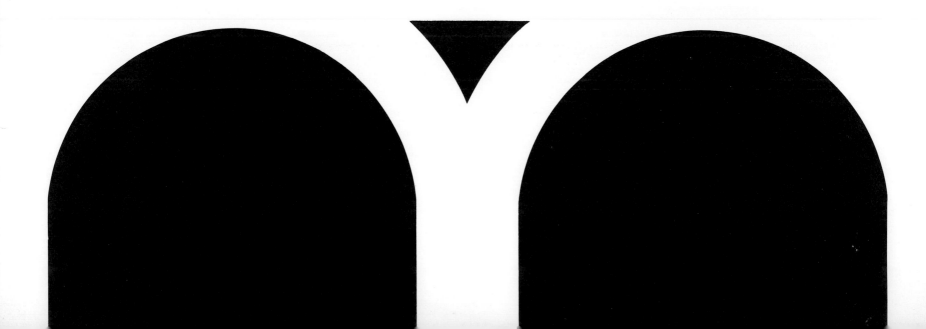

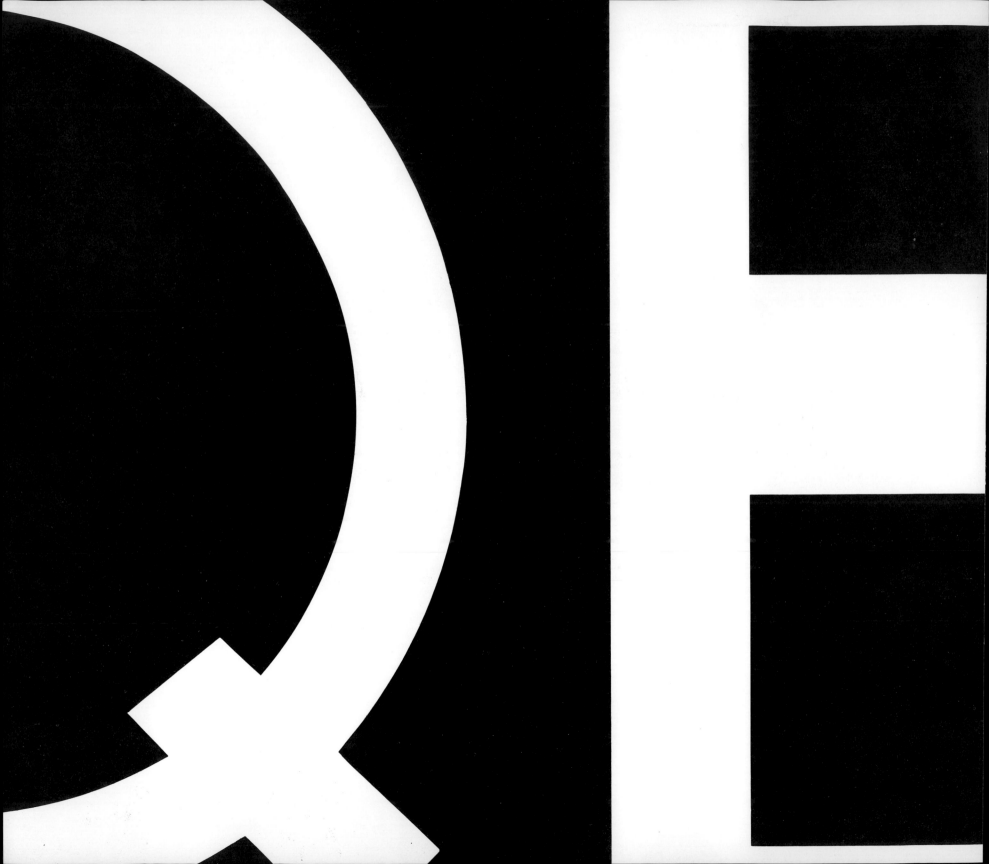

SPRING MESSAGES

Overy fiery tunnels in the wake of worms
Popaliths of April bring
Amber candles on the pines of spring.

Over amber candles on the pines of spring

Arcturus   Vega   Spica   swing
in a triangle of gold   of blue   of white,

The triangle of spring night.

What makes a message be a message
of a terpene ring
Is IN   amber candles on the pines of spring.
What makes Arcturus   Vega   Spica   bright
WAS in   Galaxies in spring night.

What told the light to tell the eye
to shape what shone

May turn a triangle . . . into a cone.

SECTION II   THREE CHRISTMAS CARDS

When the holidays come, are the Holy days gone?

1965 Card
1966 Card
1967 Card

CARD 1965

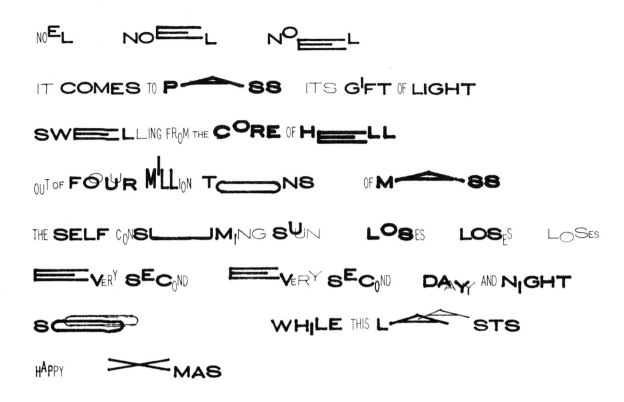

NOEL   NOEL   NOEL

IT COMES TO PASS   ITS GIFT OF LIGHT

SWELLING FROM THE CORE OF HELL

OUT OF FOUR MILLION TONS   OF MASS

THE SELF CONSUMING SUN   LOSES   LOSES   LOSES

EVERY SECOND   EVERY SECOND   DAY AND NIGHT

SO   WHILE THIS LASTS

HAPPY XMAS

CARD 1966

WHAT HALF DESIGNED.....HALF RANDOM FLEW

IS BRINGING YOU A YULE TIME HUE

OUR INTENTION SHARES ITS CALCULATED WAYS

OUR SPONTANEITY ITS UNPREDICTED SPLAYS

AND BOTH TRANSCRIBE OUR WISH OF CHEEER

FOR YOU .....NEXT YEAR

CARD 1967

WHEN NIGHTS SHRINK IN LOONGer DAYS

MAY YOUR WASSAIL REMIND YOU

HOW FAN-TAILed MAMAS MARCH OUT OF SUPERMARKET SWARMS

WITH SHARDS OF TEMPLES IN THEIR ARMS

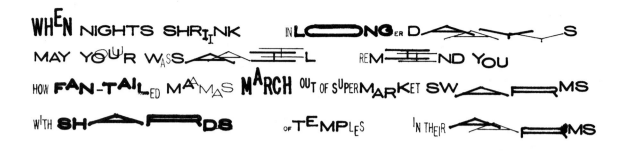

WHEN NIGHTS SHRINK IN LOONGer DAYS

MAY YOUR WASSAIL REMIND YOU

HOW TO FIND THRU OPEN WATERS OF YOUR IRIS

ELOQUENCE . . . . . AND LIGHT

IN LIMBS OF OSIRIS

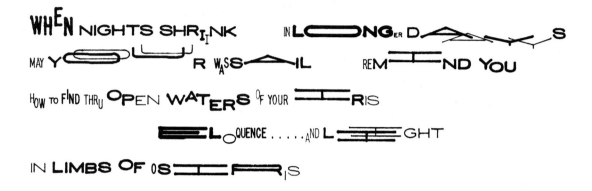

NOR FORGET THE QUESTION OF THE EARTH

TURNING TOWARD REBIRTH

IN THE MATRIX OF YOUR MIND

IS CHRIST A SWEET . . . . . OR BITTER RIND

SEPWIDGITTINKNUL

IF YOU COULD PREDICT THE ONSET OF YOUR ADVENT........

INTO YOUR N⟨⟩WHERE OF N⟨⟩WHEN

YOU WOULD NOT LAUGH WHEN YOU HEARD THE BELL

OF THAT GALLOPY LITTLE BEDPAN JOCKY SEPWIDJIT TINKNUL

IS WHAT BAFFLES ENTROPY THE UNIVERSE'S NOISE

SO YOU CANNOT HEAR THE KNELL

IN SEPWIDJIT TINKNUL'S BELL

SEPWIDJIT TINKNUL SEPWIDJIT TINKNUL

IF THE DATE SEPWIDJIT TINKNUL KNELLS

WERE KNOWN

IN ADVANCE

CUTTERS FOR MONEY WOULDN'T SELL

A STONE

FOR THE PAST

39

HYMN TO THE RAT RAC

WILL TH**EY** CASTRATE C**O**S TIGAN

INDEED   INDEED   INDEED

W**I**LL THEY CASTRATE C**O**STIGAN

I**N**D**EE**D   I**N**D**EE**D   I**N**D**EE**D

C**A**N THEY CASTRATE C**O**S TIGAN

WHY **NOT**   WHY **NOT**   WHY **N**O**T**

CAN TH**EY**   C**A**STRATE C**O**S TIGAN

WH**Y**   NOT   WH**Y**   NOT   WH**Y** N**O**T

SHOULD TH**EY**   CASTRATE C**O**S TIGAN

WHO **E**LSE WHO **E**LSE   WHO   **E**LSE

SH**OU**LD THEY C**A**STRATE C**O**S TIGAN

WH**O** KN**O**WS   WH**O** KN**O**WS

WH**O** KN**O**WS

M**U**S**T** THEY C**A**STRATE   C**O**S TIGAN

OH**NO**   OH**N**O   O**H** N**O**

QUARK

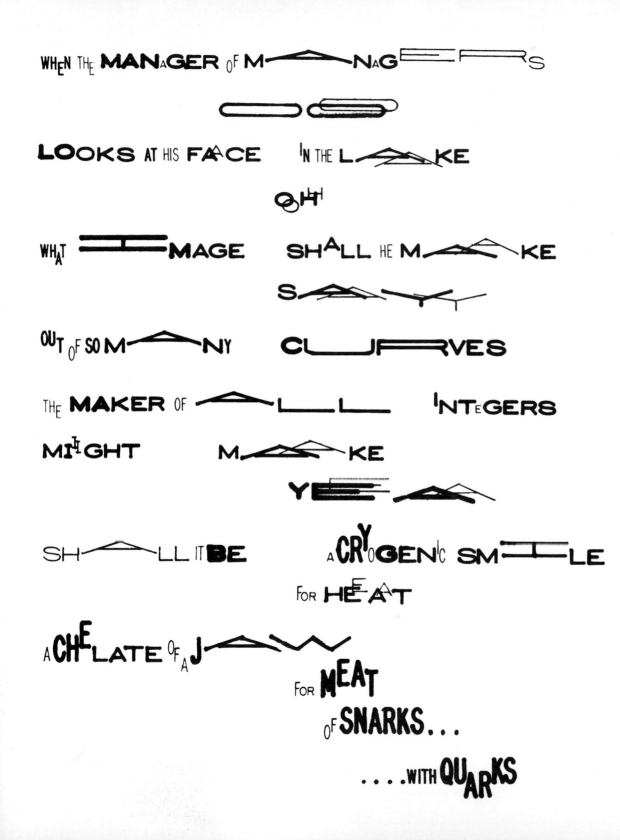

WHEN THE **MAN**AGER OF M A NAGERS

LOOKS AT HIS **FACE** IN THE LAKE

OH

WHAT IMAGE SHALL HE MAKE

SAY

OUT OF SO MANY CURVES

THE **MAKER** OF ALL INTEGERS

MIGHT MAKE

YEA

SHALL IT **BE** A CRYOGENIC SMILE

FOR HEAT

A CHELATE OF A JAW

FOR MEAT

OF SNARKS...

....WITH QUARKS

VOICES OF THE BOUYS

Tightly tied as if wired to a solid bottom,
Swaying with the waves,
Repeating the beats of the deeps,
The noise of the tirelessly tossing buoys
Uncoils on,
On a sea-widening of horizon.
The tonged recoils of the noise of the buoys,
Drawn with the long clong that iron hawsers
    haul
Are always calling,
Always calling,
How this rising-falling
Stays stably based upon an unchanged origin,
Beneath the sweeps.
It seems to be a lean and mineral tree
Recoiling from the buoyant whorls of
    salty water
In the dawns beneath the sea;
A sidewise leaning and a loil,
Whose winnowing seems unweariedly to be
    revealing
Blue winds keeling
Through the interior in the sphered marine.
Yet these unwearied clongings,
When in period pealings,
These turquoise noises of the buoys
Loiter on in spite of lost spawn,
In spite of all the lost oil wasted on the bay,
In spite of crimes, wars, wrongs,
The cries, snorts, tossed bodies of bleeding
    seamen
Destroyed in the deeps,
Still the buoys are always buoyant,
Always clonging on, gonging on,
Through fogs,
Through storms,
Warning of dangers on the way;
Pleading with their pealing,
Enjoining all who sail
To hear the toiling voice within the tongs,
Forged by peoples, nations, races from all
    climes;
Assayed in fire, refined and crystallized from
    mines,
Voicing Ahoy! Ahoy!
Alloyed chains of labor's ties!
Accouterments of time, change, song,
Silver chiming coins of continents,
Voice of Man—upon the seas!

BEHIND THE FACE OF THE WATER

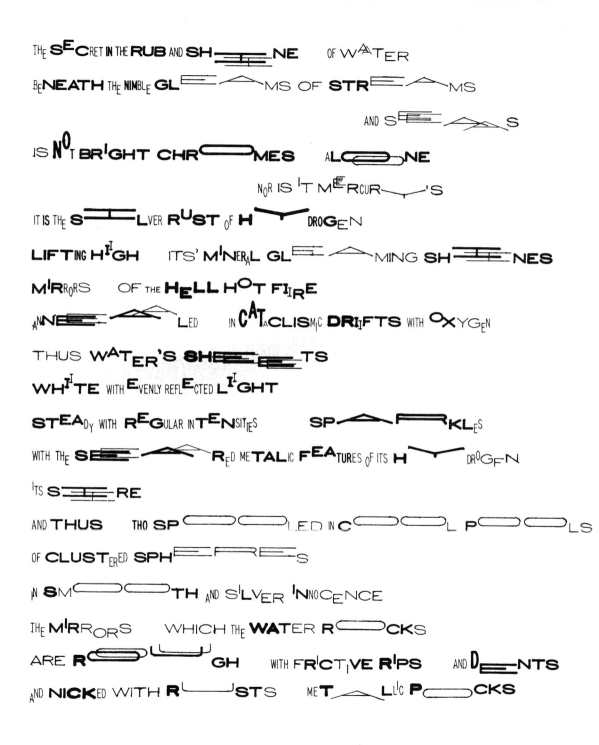

The secret in the rub and shine of water
Beneath the nimble gleams of streams and
     seas
Is not bright chrome's alone, nor is it
     mercury's.
It is the silver rust of hydrogen
Lifting high its mineral gleaming shines,
Mirrors of the hell-hot fire,
Annealed in cataclysmic drifts with oxygen:
Thus water's sheets,
White with evenly reflected light,
Steady with regular intensities,
Sparkles with the seared metallic
Features of its hydrogen, its sire.
And, thus, though spooled in cool pools
Of clustered spheres in smooth and silver
     innocense,
The mirrors, which the water rocks,
Are rough with frictive rips and dents,
And nicked with rust's metallic pocks.

STONY RIVER

UNDER THE VEIL

   UNDER THE PURL

OF **HUM-DRUMMED** WVES   IN SLOW-ROLLED AIR

GR**EAT** SLEEP **WASH**ED **MON**OT**O**NES

BROUGHT S**O**METHING OF THOSE L**O**NG-SPILLED W**A**YS ON ME

SP**AWNED** IN THE SP**E**LL

   UNDER THE SW**I**RL

D**OW**N   I SL**E**PT DR**I**FTING IN THE IN**CE**SS**ANT** TR**I**CKLE IN THE FL**U**X OF R**IV**ERS

ON **O**LD **FAHM-M**O**O**DS

   BLOWN THRU **RAIN** LIPS OF R**I**FFS

   WH**IR**LED FROM BELOW FL**OW**S

      C**OO**LED **OV**ER **WA**TER W**I**SPED **ST**O**NES

   ON SH**O**ALS OF THE ESOPUS

R**I**VER OF CH**A**NGE

   R**I**VER OF **FAB**LES

      R**I**VER OF DR**O**NED F**O**AMS

Under the veil,
    Under the purl,
        of hum-drummed waves in
            slow-rolled air,
Great sleep-washed monotones brought
    something of those long-spilled
    ways on me.
Spawned in the spell,
    Under the swirl,
Down, I slept, drifting in the incessant trickle
    in the flux of rivers,
On old Fahm-moods blown through rain-lips
    of riffs,
Whirled from below flows cooled over
    water-wisped stones on shoals of the
    Esopus
River of change,
    River of fables,
        River of droned foams.

STONY RIVER

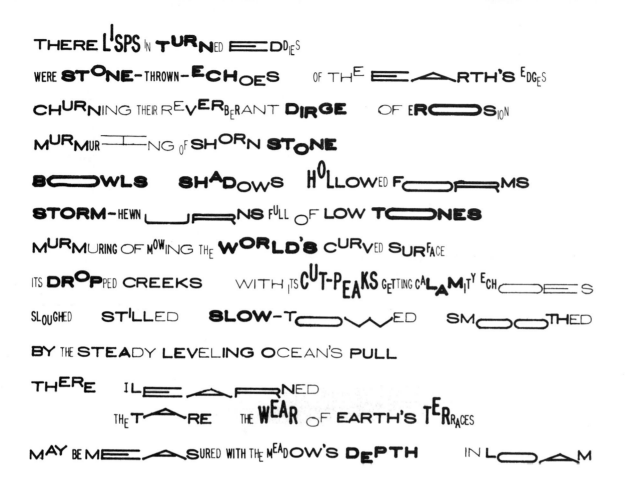

There, lisps in turnededdies were stone-
thrown echoes of the earth's edges;
Churning their reverberant dirge of erosion,
Murmuring of shorn-stone, bowls, shadows,
hollowed forms, storm-hewn urns full
of low tones,
Its dropped creeks with its cut peaks getting
calamity echoes
Sloughed, stilled, slow-toned, smoothed
By the steady- leveling ocean's pull.
There, learned: the tare, the wear of
earth's terraces
May be measured with the meadow's depth
in loam.

STONY RIVER

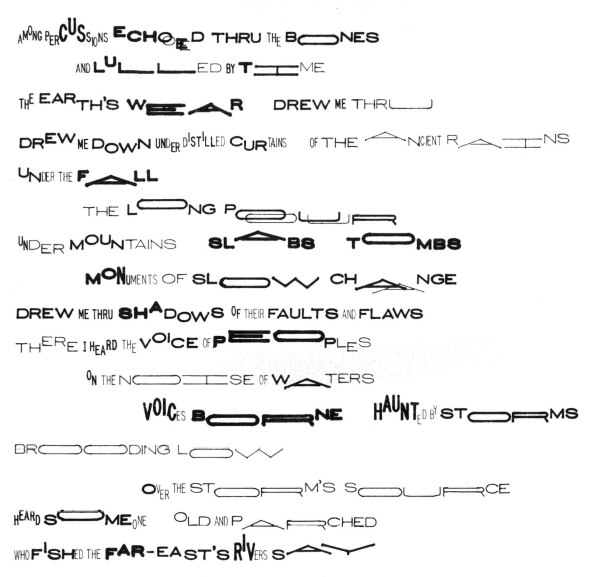

Among percussions echoed through the
   bones and lulled by time,
The earth's wear drew me through, drew
   me down
Under distilled curtains of the ancient rains,
Under the fall,
   the long pour,
Under mountains, slabs, tombs, monuments
   of slow change,
Drew me through shadows of their faults
   and flaws.
There, I heard the voice of peoples on the
   noise of waters,
Voices borne, haunted by storms:
   Brooding low over the storms' source;
Heard someone, old and parched, who
   fished the Far East's rivers say:
"Thoughts on water grow all bearded."

SECTION IV   FLIGHT FROM THE CITIES

The North Wind
Inside the Snow
Dirge of the Cold
Wood Winds
Crows
Tin Rain
The Raccoon

THE NORTH WIND

When gloom of winter evening first pulls in
The North Wind goes to bed with the
   Old Woman.

When moans from cedar woods begin
   to thin—
Oh! The North Wind goes to bed with
   the Old Woman,
Who in her hood withdrew.

INSIDE THE SNO

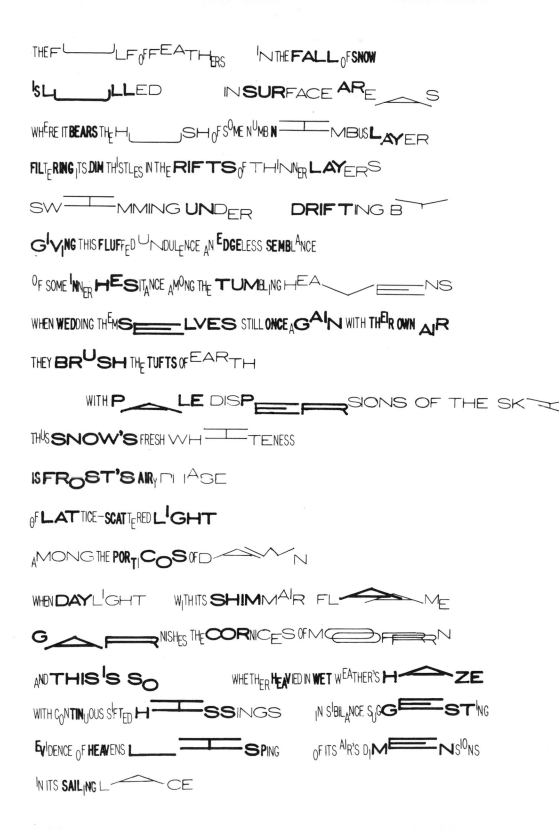

The fulf of feathers in the fall of snow
Is lulled in surface areas where
It bears the hush of some numb nimbus layer
Filtering its dimthistles in the rifts of thinner
    layers,
Swimming under, drifting by;
Giving this fluffed undulance an edgeless
    semblance
Of some inner hesitance among the tumbling
    heavens when,
Wedding themselves still once again with
    their own air,
They brush the tufts of earth with pale
    dispersions of the sky.

Thus snows fresh whiteness is frost's airy
    phase
Of lattice-scattered light among the porticos
    of dawn
When daylight with its shimmair flame
Garnishes the cornices of morn.
And this is so—whether heavied in wet
    weather's haze
With continuous sifted hissings in sibilance
    suggesting
Evidence of Heaven's lisping of its air's
    dimensions in its sailing lace,

59

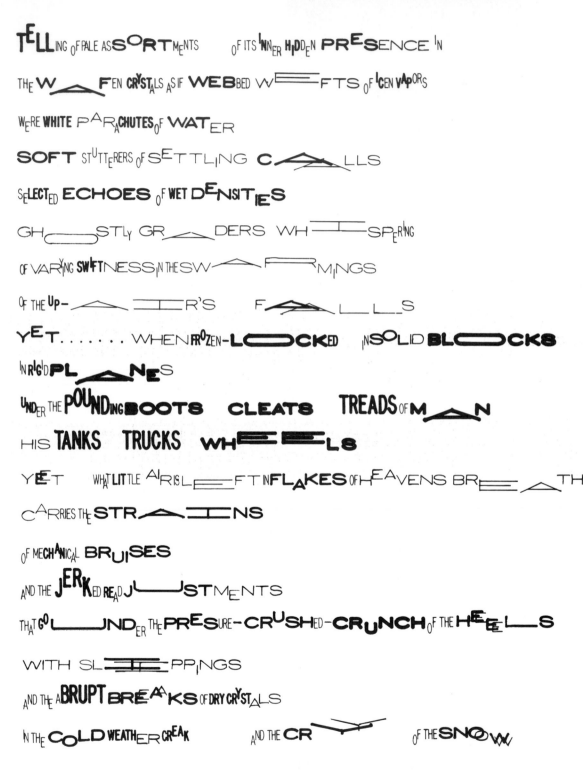

Telling of pale assortments of its inner
    hidden presence in
The wafen crystals as if webbed wefts of
    icen vapors were
White parachutes of water, soft stutterers of
    settling-calls,
Selected echoes of wet densities; ghostly
    graders whispering
Of varying swiftness in the swarmings of the
    up-air's falls.

Yet . . . . .
when frozen-locked in solid blocks in rigid
    planes

Under the pounding boots, cleats, treads of
    man,
his tanks, trucks, wheels,

Yet what little air is left in flakes of Heaven's
    breath
carries the strains

Of mechanical bruises,
and the jerked readjustments that go

Under the pressure-crushed-crunch of
    the heels . . . .

With slippings
and the abrupt breaks of dry crystals

In the cold weather creak . . . and the cry of
    the snow.

DIRGE OF THE COL

FOLLOWING LONELY CLOUDS OF SOUND

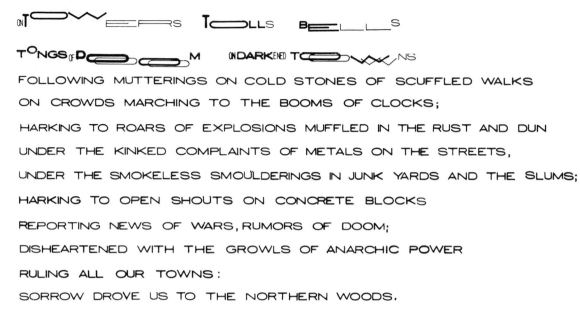

ON TOWERS TOLLS BELLS

TONGS OF DOOM ON DARKENED TOWNS

FOLLOWING MUTTERINGS ON COLD STONES OF SCUFFLED WALKS

ON CROWDS MARCHING TO THE BOOMS OF CLOCKS;

HARKING TO ROARS OF EXPLOSIONS MUFFLED IN THE RUST AND DUN

UNDER THE KINKED COMPLAINTS OF METALS ON THE STREETS,

UNDER THE SMOKELESS SMOULDERINGS IN JUNK YARDS AND THE SLUMS;

HARKING TO OPEN SHOUTS ON CONCRETE BLOCKS

REPORTING NEWS OF WARS, RUMORS OF DOOM;

DISHEARTENED WITH THE GROWLS OF ANARCHIC POWER

RULING ALL OUR TOWNS:

SORROW DROVE US TO THE NORTHERN WOODS.

BUT OVER THE NORTHERN WATERS PLOWED WITH OTTER,

OVER PONDS, MARSHES, LACUNAE IN COLD GROUND,

OVER THE REFUGE FROM THE TOWNS ONLY WOODSMEN KNOW

ROSE A FLOATING MOVING SOUND,

THE MOCKING CALL OF MELANCHOLIA'S CLOWNS:

THE

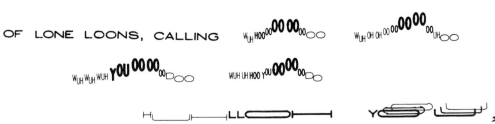

OF LONE LOONS, CALLING

WANDERERS ALONE IN THE NORTHERN GLOOM,

HUNTING IN THE COLD OF THE NORTHERN GLOOM!

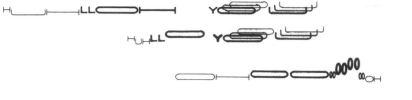

SWALLOWED, BROKEN OFF AS THOUGH SOME LONELY HUMAN

GULPING WATER,

LOSING BUBBLES THROUGH THE BLUE

WERE DROWNING ALL ALONE.

FOLLOWING FROM AUGUST ON THE OVER-PALLS OF CLOUDS ON MOUNTAINS

THROUGH THE AUTUMN RAINS,

THROUGH NOVEMBER'S COLD THROUGH THE NORTHERN SOLSTICE,

FOLLOWING THOSE DARK HOURS,

BORN IN THE STORM, MOVING THROUGH THE GLOOM,

OVER THE FROZEN SNOW,

FLOATING OVER THE FARMLESS MARSHES, OVER THE MOST UNHUMAN GROUNDS,

HOMELESS.... ROADLESS.... HUGE

BLOWN OUT OF THE HOLLOWS OF BRUTES, OUT OF THEIR HOUNDED HEARTS,

AROSE THOSE BROODING, YOWLING TONES,

THOSE LONELY RUTHFUL SOUNDS,

THE OPEN MOUTHED

HOWLS OF COYOTES AND WOLVES,

FATHERS OF WARNING, LOW THROATED, CHORDED TO RUMBLE,

NOSE WHOOING TO THE MOON,

NOSE BEADING THE MOON.

BROODING ON THE SLOWNESS, THE LOW PITCH, THE LONG DRAWN TONE

OF THOSE PURSUING VOLUMES OF SOUND

I PONDER WHETHER THEIR SLOW MOTIONS ARE NOT UNCONSCIOUS KNOWLEDGE

HOW OUT OF THE SLOWING DOWN OF ALL MOTION,

OUT OF THE COOLINGS OF SLOWED MOTIONS

GROW THE COLDEST VOLUMES IN THE UNIVERSE....

WHERE ALL POWER IS LOST

AMONG UNKNOWN ZONES OF INSCRUTABLE GLOOM

LOOMING BEYOND THE OUTERMOST STARS,

BOUNDING AN OMINOUS DARKNESS;

AND I WONDER WHETHER THOSE FORLORN CALLS OF THE STORM,

THOSE LONELY CLOUDS OF SOUND

ARE NOT COPYING THE LOWERED TONES OF OUR SORROW

OVER OUR LOSS OF POWER TO THE COLD;

ARE NOT MOCKING OUR MOANS FOR OUR OWN SLOWING—DOWNS

ON GOING ALONE TO THE VOLUME AND HUGE OF ULTIMATE COLD

ON THE SLOW MOTION OF UNBOUNDED AND ALL—ENSHROUDING DARKNESS:

WHETHER THE OH OOSS OO OH OH WUH OH OH OO OO OOOO OO UH OO

CALLS OF THE LOONS,

FORLORN, LONELY, BORN IN THE STORM,

OR THE AHH OHOOSO

HOWLS OF COYOTES AND WOLVES,

OR THE SOUNDS OF TOWERS TOLLS BELLS

TONGS OF DOOM ON DARKENED TOWNS

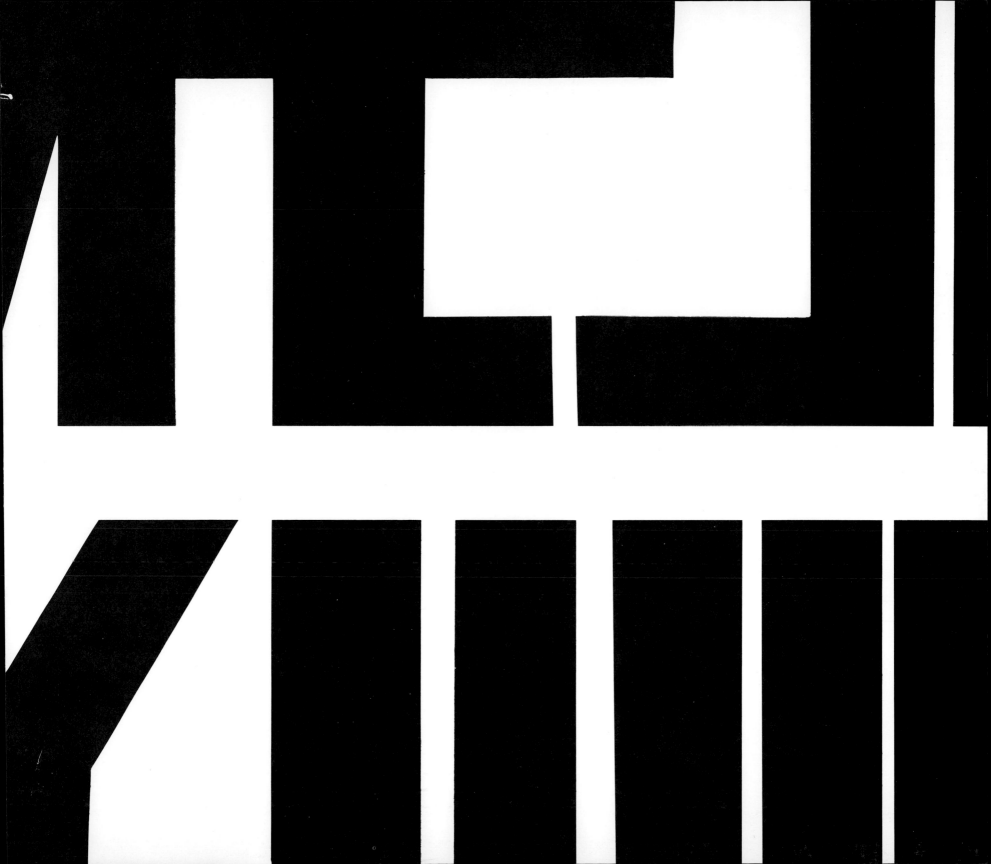

WOOD WIND

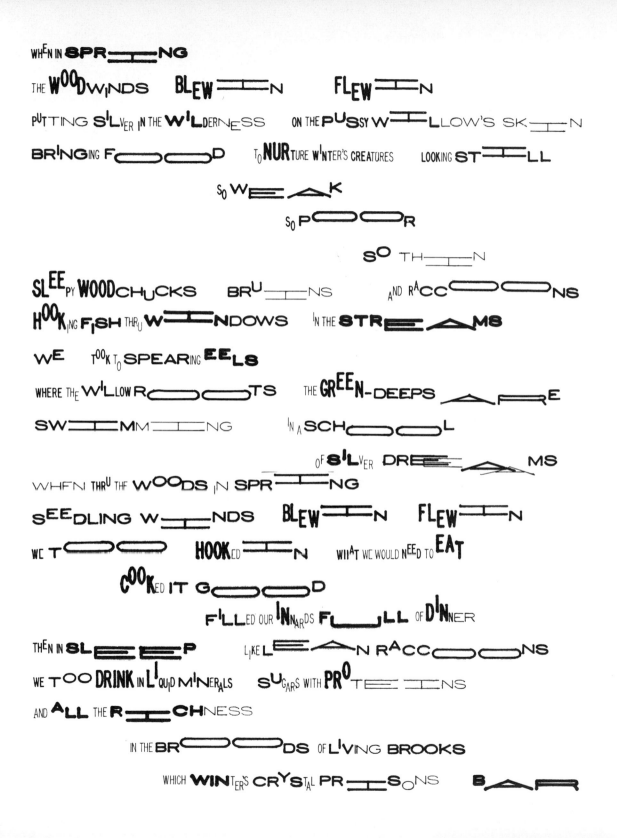

When in Spring
The wood winds blew-in, flew-in,
Putting silver in the wilderness on the
    pussy willow's skin;
Bringing food to nurture Winter's creatures,
    looking still
        So weak,
            So poor,
                So thin:
Sleepy woodchucks, bruins,
And racoons hooking fish through windows
    in the streams,
We took to spearing eels.
Where the willow roots the green deeps are,
Swimming in a school of silver dreams.

When through the woods in Spring
Seedling winds blew-in, flew-in,
We, too, hooked-in what we would need
    to eat;
        cooked it good,
            filled our innards full of dinner.
Then in sleep, like lean raccoons,
We, too, drink-in liquid minerals, sugars
    and proteins,
And all the richness
    in the broods of living brooks
        Which Winter's crystal prisons   bar.

CROW

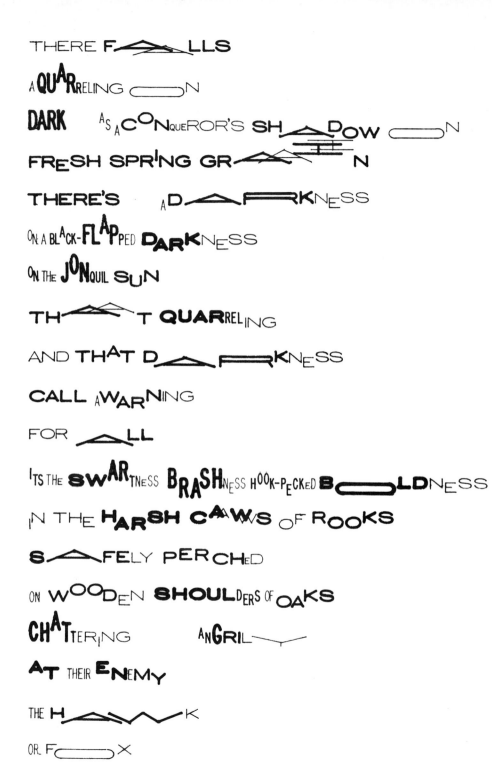

There falls
A quarreling on,
Dark as a conquerer's shadow on
Fresh Spring Grain.

There's a darkness on,
A black-flapped darkness on
the jonquil sun.

That quarreling and that darkness
Call a warning,

For . . . all.

Its the swartness, brashness, hook-pecked
   boldness
In the harsh caws of rooks,

Safely perched
On wooden shoulders of oaks,
Chattering angrily,

At their enemy,

The hawk,

or fox.

TIN RA

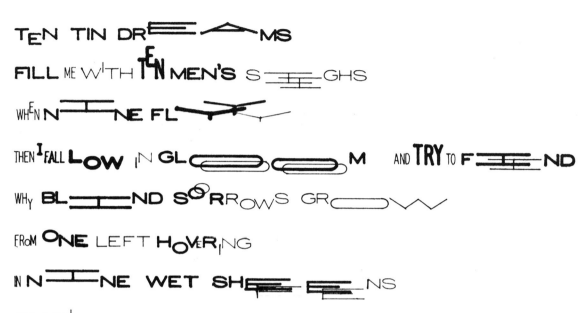

Ten tin dreams
Stem in the rain.

I try to who knows why.

Ten tin dreams
Fill me with ten men's sighs.

When nine fly,
Then I fall low in gloom
and try to find why blind sorrows grow
from one left hovering in

Nine wet sheens,
On tin.

THE RACCOO

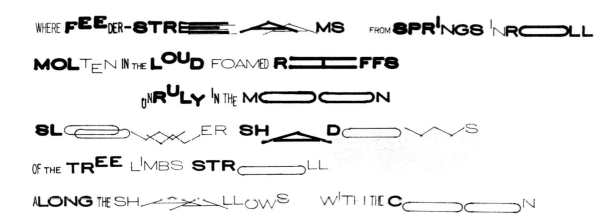

We saw the coon roaming in pools
To scoop with claws his moon-wink trout,
Washing Procyon in the stream;
Where only winds, besides his nimble paws,
Spread a rippling sheen.

Where feeder-streams from springs inroll,
Molten in the loud-foamed riffs, unruly in
    the moon,
Slower shadows of the tree limbs stroll
Along the shallows with the coon.

VOICES IN THE VIOLIN

WITH A QUIET SIGH OF NEED

THE STRING-WINDS OF THE VIOLINS

BEGIN THE SINUOUS SHIVERINGS WHICH PLEAD

I SIGHING PINE OF NEED   I SIGH OF NEED

THEN A TRILLING   ON A FINER **TIGHT**ER LINE

RISES   IN A **FELINE** VISCERAL **WHINE**

WITH A **SWEET**   STRING-TINGLED KEENING

SHRILLING THIN   AND HIGH   AND FINE

UNTIL THE **FIBRES** QUIVER   WITH THE **PIER**CING **MEA**NING

OF THE **NEAR** HYS**TER**IA   WHICH IS TRYING TO CRY   IN

THE **FEMININE VI**OLENCE   OF THE VIOLIN

I CRY TO BREED   I CRY TO BREED
ON UNTAUT THONGS   THEN THROBS A **HOARSE**NESS

DROPPING **LOW**

ON THE PRO**LONG**ED TWONG

OF LONG UNDIVIDED **STRINGS**

S**O**BBING

OF THE **COARSE**   SONG-DRAWN **HORSE**-HAIR BOW

THEN THE **VI**OLENCE   OF THE VIOLINS

REBE**GINS**

TO SPEED ITS **VI**BRANT **HIGH**INGS   FROM THE WHITE-STEAMED AND THE KILN-**DRIED** LIGNINS

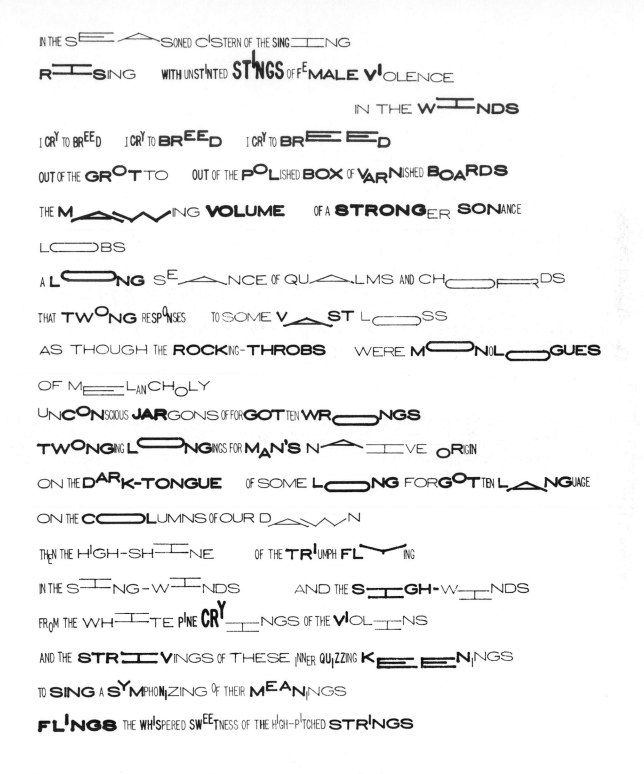

IN THE SEASONED CISTERN OF THE SINGING

RISING   WITH UNSTINTED STINGS OF FEMALE VIOLENCE

                                        IN THE WINDS

I CRY TO BREED   I CRY TO BREED   I CRY TO BREED

OUT OF THE GROTTO   OUT OF THE POLISHED BOX OF VARNISHED BOARDS

THE MAWING VOLUME   OF A STRONGER SONANCE

LOBS

A LONG SEANCE OF QUALMS AND CHOORDS

THAT TWONG RESPONSES   TO SOME VAST LOSS

AS THOUGH THE ROCKING-THROBS   WERE MONOLOGUES

OF MELANCHOLY

UNCONSCIOUS JARGONS OF FORGOTTEN WRONGS

TWONGING LONGINGS FOR MAN'S NATIVE ORIGIN

ON THE DARK-TONGUE   OF SOME LONG FORGOTTEN LANGUAGE

ON THE COLUMNS OF OUR DAWN

THEN THE HIGH-SHINE   OF THE TRIUMPH FLYING

IN THE SING-WINDS   AND THE SIGH-WINDS

FROM THE WHITE PINE CRYINGS OF THE VIOLINS

AND THE STRIVINGS OF THESE INNER QUIZZING KEENINGS

TO SING A SYMPHONIZING OF THEIR MEANINGS

FLINGS THE WHISPERED SWEETNESS OF THE HIGH-PITCHED STRINGS

INTO PIERCING QUIVERINGS   WHICH EXCEED IN SPEED

THE PREVIOUS PERIODS WHICH THE V═══BRANCE RINGS

TO RISE STILL-SHRILLER SWIFTER ══N THE SKY⌄

L══NGERING WITH A S══ZY-T══MBRE IN THEIR LIFTINGS

UNTIL THE CLIMBING OF THIS SINEWIZING ST══NGS

ITS KEEN LEAPING SIEZING CR⌄

I CRY TO BR══EED   I CRY TO BR══EED

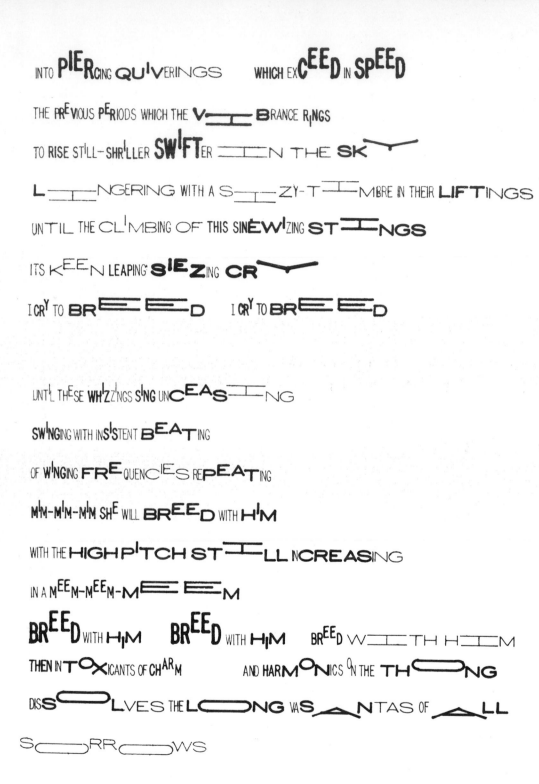

UNTIL THESE WHIZZINGS SING UNCEASING

SWINGING WITH INSISTENT BEATING

OF WINGING FREQUENCIES REPEATING

MIM-MIM-MIM SHE WILL BREED WITH HIM

WITH THE HIGH PITCH ST══LL INCREASING

IN A MEEM-MEEM-M══EEM

BREED WITH HIM   BREED WITH HIM   BREED WITH HIM

THEN INTOXICANTS OF CHARM   AND HARMONICS ON THE THONG

DISSOLVES THE LONG VASANTAS OF ALL

SORROWS

IN ADAGIOS OF SOFT SONG

SONGS OF CALMNESS

DRAWING CALMS OF SOLACE FROM LONG THOUGHTS

SOLITARY THOUGHTS

THOUGHTS SO SOMBRE AND SO SOUGHT FOR

FOR SO LONG

THEY FALL IN DARKNESS ON THE CARMINE GARDENS OF OUR ORGANS

AND WANDER IN THE HAUNTS OF CONCEPTS

IN THE SHADOWS OF THE BODY'S WALLS

THERE THE VIOLIN'S SONGS GROW STRONG

THEY THROB THEY SAW

(WITHIN THOSE HALLS OF MORTAL POWER THOSE CARNAL

VAULTS)

A SOFT AUTONOMOUS UNLOCKING OF OUR DAWNS

WITH WARM UNKNOTINGS OF THE BONDS OF THOUGHTS

AND THEY VAUNT HOW THIS INCARNATE POWER

WITH ITS PROMISE OF A SHARPER CONSCIOUSNESS OF SORROW

SHALL ASSAULT ALL WALLS UPON THE MORROW

LYRIC FOR A FLUTE

The little peep, peep seeps
of a winter creek
beneath a wooden bridge,

Blowing through the wood blue-peeps,

Repeatedly reveals,

(in keeping up these drips and leaks
   of little silver bibbling beads)

How aerial echoed spheres

Who will swing floo-ee, floo-ee,

Who-She? Who-He? Whoo-You?

Who will swoop, then kick?

Who will coast, then flit, loop and leap
in hoops and rings on peaks of toes?

Who'll be tickled with a queer-kinked tune
Those teak timbered overtones balloon?

Who will limn their azure-looped agility
lilting with atmospheric elasticity?

To-whom, to-whom . . . to-whom
do these aerially blue and fluid tunes
bring boobling dreams of tone-blown beings
breathing soluble imaginings?

Who hears in these quick-dimplings of the
   winds
a wooing whistling,
ear-wooing you to feel fluid
and free
as the flittery-moving, everywhere fluencies
   of air

Whose keys begin with echoed peep, peep,
   seeps
beneath the ice on winter creeks

And finish with the flute's queer-kinked toots
and cool liquidities,
flittering
      woo-ees, floo-ees, woo-ees, floo-ees?

Cooly lift balloons in beats,

Moving
      through the long, lean
sealed-in-rooms of tubes,
bowls, closed-in-cupulas, flues,
pipes, booths, keys, and flutes,

And the blue-water bottle of the air
Between
    the lowered flow of freezing creeks

And the frozen dome each streamlet keeps
with the crystalline expansion
of its icen sheets.

With the little peep, peep, peeps,

Boobling through the winter creeks,

We hear the cool clear toots
in queer kinked tunes of flutes,
blowing
    floo-ee, floo-ee . . .

With acoustical simplicity.

Through reeds within the licker's tooth

Each Lilliputian tibal bead
leaps with a clear and silvery speed
in a series of
    floo-ees, floo-ees.
These, pursuing, plea to you and me,
(to both the old and youth)

Who will flee with me? Whoo-You?

Who will dance to these cool toots,

Who will stoop and leap in tune,

Who will, please? Whoo-You?

Whoo-He? Whoo-She? Whoo-You?

Who will go floo-ee with me?

Who will swing floo-ee with me?

FINAL

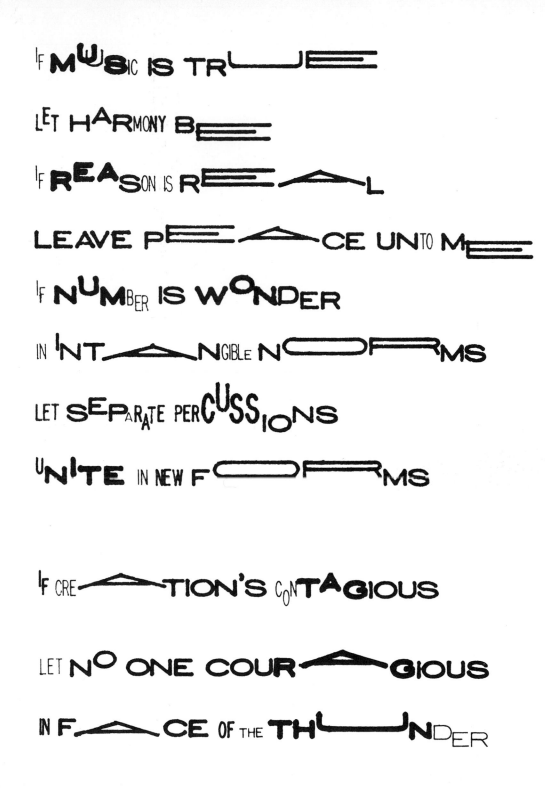

IF MUSIC IS TRUE

LET HARMONY BE

IF REASON IS REAL

LEAVE PEACE UNTO ME

IF NUMBER IS WONDER

IN INTANGIBLE NORMS

LET SEPARATE PERCUSSIONS

UNITE IN NEW FORMS

IF CREATION'S CONTAGIOUS

LET NO ONE COURAGIOUS

IN FACE OF THE THUNDER

OF OUR WORLD GOING UNDER

NOT SEEEEK IN ANARCHY

THE ULTIMATE UNITY

OF SCIENCE.......AND SYMMETRY

APPENDIX

Energy levels written into these poems and their relations to reality.

Two compositions in this book were created with attention to the energy levels of speech as thematic information. "Towards Lyra and the Swan," written between 1963 and 1964, was presented to the Linguistic, phonetic and Voice Interest group meeting at the Speech Association of America Convention in 1965 at New York City. That it was well received by a critical group increased my interest in this poem. "The Dirge of the Cold" was written between 1940 and 1942 under miserable conditions of poverty, insecurity, and the madness of World War II. The City of New York presented it on its radio station WNYC in the late spring of 1942. This poem always impressed me as the best composition I have written and the most far reaching in the problems it raised.

The images in "The Dirge of the Cold" were visual associations that "low" vowels such as [a] in [father], [o] in [cold], [v] in [hood], and the diphthong [av] in [how] generated in the mind of the poet. Since [a→o→v], when spoken rapidly one after the other, blend into the sound of the diphthong [av], the rhythm of the poem develops from the conspicuous redundancy of its low vowel tones. A "low" pitched vowel is one near the bottom of a scale of vowel tones judged relatively lower in level by listeners to the heights of tones in whispered vowels. Occasionally for contrast or in the weak less audible syllables "high" whisper-pitched vowels appear: [i] as in [see], [I] as in [hit],

[E] as in [red]. Their appearance in unstressed syllables reduces their tonal prominence in favor of the "low" vowelled syllables. For the sceptical reader, Figure I, contrasts the high frequency of occurrence of "low" vowels in this poem with the statistics for their average occurrence in American English.

The visual associations that clustered around the low vowels produced sets of voiced-images. Search for a pattern with both subjective and objective meaning united these disparate clusters of vocal images into the theme of the poem: similarities between lowering of frequency, lowering of pitch, lowering of kinetic energy, with feeling enervated and "low" and a let down of emotion.

Does the kinetic energy of the low overtone vowels support the energy theme of this poem? The poet heard the low pitches of his designed-to-sound-low vowels, but, objectively, were they really weaker in internal energy than the high pitched vowels? There is an equation for energy of the acoustic wave that strikes the listener's ear with both frequency in vibration and amplitude of sound pressure. This total energy in ergs is the product of N^2 multiplied by A^2 where N means number of vibrations per second and A is amplitude. For our problem the other variables in this equation are irrelevant. Which contributed more energy: the amplitude or the frequency of the vowel? To answer this question two passages of prose were given to twelve students in the Speech and Hearing laboratory of Temple University. One passage was written entirely with the "low" vowels

FIGURE 1.

Redundancy of "low" vowels in "Dirge of the Cold" compared with low vowel occurrences in American English

FREQUENCY OF OCCURRENCE	"Dirge of the Cold" Poem	French, Carter and Koenig based on telephone conversation	Peter Denes based on Phonetic Readers	G. Dewey based on newspapers
$\dfrac{av}{\text{all vowels}}$	8.3	1.69	2.0	1.6
$\dfrac{\text{stressed } av}{\text{all stressed vowels}}$	13.9	2.2	3.4	— — — —
$\dfrac{\text{stressed } ɔ+a+o+v}{\text{all stressed syllables}}$	40.1	24.51	18.83	— — — —
$\dfrac{\text{all } ɔ+a+o+v}{\text{all syllables}}$	24.8	18.58	12.00	16.7
$\dfrac{\text{stressed } av+a+o+v}{\text{all stressed syllables}}$	47.9	19.33	21.26	— — — —
$\dfrac{\text{all } av+a+o+v}{\text{all syllables}}$	34.1	19.33	21.26	11.7

of the "Dirge of the Cold," the other passage, exclusively, with "high" vowels [i], [I], [e], [E] as in Keep, Kip, Kate, Kep. The audio signals were sent to an optical oscillograph (Honeywell Model 2106), from which the fundamental pitch measurements were obtained. The speech signals were transmitted by a high quality condenser microphone (Bruel Kjaer, Model 4131) amplified, and sent to a graphic level recorder (Bruel Kjaer Model 2305) from which overall RMS amplitude readings were obtained. RMS=root mean square.

The conclusions of this test were inconclusive. The "low" vowelled passage averaged +5Db higher and —7Hz (cps) lower than the "high" vowel passage. The energy difference between the "pitch" and amplitude components worked out to be 5%. Minor energy differences in continuous tradings between these two energy variables would make little auditory differences to listeners insofar as listeners were "objective" recorders of independent acoustic waves. But they were not "objective" recorders. The subjective story is the way the human ear and brain screens and perceives and categorizes a few acoustic patterns out of many in the flow of language. Whether the impact of amplitude or of tonal frequency will dominate the auditory impression of a poem will depend on the relative power of the acoustic cues for stress in the poet's native language. The acoustic correlates that cue the rhythms of American English are: amplitude, time duration, and the fundamental frequency of "pitch." These are the physical components of stress patterns. The question is: which of these is the strongest cue for hearing the rhythms of English?

Linguists and the more experimental phoneticians over the last fifty years have concluded that pitch carries more information than amplitude. We have in mind experiments of Dwight Bollinger, Daniel Jones and others that assessed pitch as a stronger cue than amplitude for perceiving speech contours and levels of the voice. Spectographs by P. Delattre, measurements by P. Lieberman and information display analyses by I. Pollack as well as our own investigations all support the conclusion that pitch is a slightly more powerful cue than amplitude. It is this extra sensitivity in receptivity to the pitch of English speech, whether fundamental pitch or mean overtone pitch, that gives reader-speakers of the vowels in this poem the impression of "lowness" in energy. This impression overrides the $+5Db$ higher mean amplitude level of "The Dirge of the Cold." However, the sense of this "lowness" in pitch and mood is identified again and reinforced by the meanings of words throughout the composition. The explicitness of the theme consolidates the energy message of the prosody. The cultural achievement is that energy concepts which engineer our civilization and shape our vision of our night sky and our existence in depths of space have been subjectivized in the integration of a poem with its physical medium. Although this creation is surely minor compared with Kepler's success in formulating the 3rd law of planetary motion I know a little something of the elation he felt after the solution of his problem: "If you forgive me, I rejoice; if you are angry, I can bear it; the die is cast, the book is written . . . etc."

"Towards Lyra and the Swan" with its storm rising in the East, with its dying down tones and quasi chimpanzee cries is another experiment to write energy levels into poetry. Here, a set of artificial cues that tell the reader to speak on specified levels of amplitude, fundamental pitch and periods of duration simplifies the problem of transforming the fixed traits of vowels into audible patterns. The author's intent for performance becomes visible. It remains clear and unequivocable even though the reader disregards it.

The energy theme of this poem is the well known onset-decay curve that characterizes the cycle of aging and all natural processes with power contours that rise to their peak far more rapidly than they fall to zero.

Since the world may end with a bang as likely as with a whimper, the onset-decay curve is less universal than the energy level message in "The Dirge of the Cold." Yet, it is illuminating to see the shape of a vowel rise-fall extend through lines and the whole theme of a poem. The pervasiveness of this curve may on first sight give the impression of "emblematic" poetry where the shape of the printed poem on the page is a visual analogue of the poem's theme. Dylan Thomas' sun-dial shaped poems about the passage of time exemplifies this style. Yet, "Towards Lyra and the Swan" is not emblematic poetry. The shape of its cues are instructions to readers to speak in certain ways as well as to identify the power-time contours of events. The pattern of the print is more than an analogue; is more than an inter-

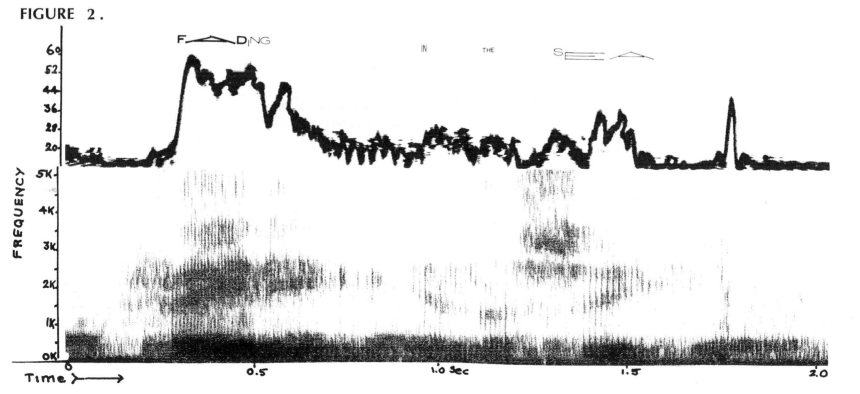

FIGURE 2.

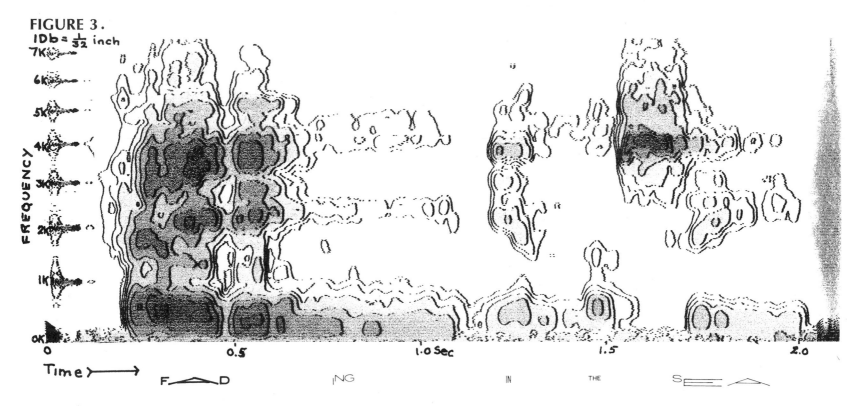

FIGURE 3.

$1Db = \frac{1}{32}$ inch

FREQUENCY

7K

6K

5K

4K

3K

2K

1K

0K

0   0.5   1.0 Sec   1.5   2.0

Time⟶   F   A   D   ING   IN   THE   S   E   A

pretive symbol: it is an operation-symbol such as [+], [—], [√], etc. Consequently the form of the print really does express the shape of the voice as the visible intent of the poet.

One of the results of an independent set of independent cues in print is the measurability of the poet's vocal intent. Did the performance show fidelity to the cues in the script? If it did, was the cue pattern a rare and unexpected form of language or was it just another stale expression of highly probable English? That these questions might be answered precisely appears in the spectrograph of one phrase taken by Dr. Lawrence Kirsta of Voice Print Inc. Here we observe the shape of the print parallel to the shape of the amplitude and overtone contours of the voice. (Figure 2-3)

It should be emphasized that the capacity of an orthography to lend itself to more exact criticism of poetic intent and performance can give no more than a post hoc critique on poetic excellence. It cannot generate the creative imagination that makes memorable poetry . . . although it might tell us in more detail why we will forget a poem.

These poems do embody some of the myth-like values discussed in the introduction. As techniques for writing about and with and for natural and man-made energy contours, hopefully, this approach will be rich as a stimulus for experimentation.

Some of the experimental work in this book was done in cooperation with Dr. Martin F. Schwartz head of research at the Temple University Speech and Hearing department and Dr. Joseph Agnello of the Speech and Hearing department of the University of Buffalo.

Notes on Three Christmas Cards

"Culture" has been rationalized as a configuration of the ways peoples imagine their existence. This approach leads to these questions: what is the substance of this kind of imagination? What activities do people share besides birth, sex, and death? What are the invariable reference points of a people's imagination, the constant experiences and values everyone understands? In the past these constant symbols of existence were always involved with the fables, myths, legends, and religions of peoples. Now all constant landmarks of history disappear in the limbo of our technological revolution. Cities are unrecognizably transformed, our countrysides vanish, rivers change their course. More powerful controls of "nature" ever accelerate these changes. Extreme specialization cuts us off from a background of common visual experience that is identifiable for most of the members of society. Under the circumstances there is little physical content in our existence that the memory of the poet can transform into universal symbols. Therefore: Christmas and New Years cards.

A Christmas or a New Years Day message is one of the few events participated in by everybody in an industrialized society. Because these holidays are determined by the motions and attitudes of the Earth in relation to the sun they really are universal events. Regretably their cosmic reality is omitted or distorted or obfuscated by the usual commercial card. All that remains is the written reminder "I think of you." Consequently, Christmas or New Years Day cards permit the poet to express his own vision of existence, his own personal outlook in terms of a universal event—a personal greeting synchronized by a cosmic change that determines our existence.

The 1967 New Years card is of special interest. It establishes two clear reference points for the poetic imagination: the holiday and a graphic imagery that is partly random. It is an unorganized picture on paper that at once gives the poet an image potential for writing his own poem and at the same time for establishing a common visual reference for himself and his readers. It is the explicitness of the unexpected in a graphic display of randomness that gives this creative opportunity. The background shared by the poet with his readers is reduced to a picture characterized by disorder. Readers can follow whatever new order is contributed by the poetry. All the stimuli and inspirations to associate personal vision or subjective attitudes or individualized conceptions begin with an event on a piece of paper that the reader can see. The inception of the poem is freed from ignorance, the uncertainties and ambiguities of reference that characterize our artificial environment. Immediate imagery has displaced the cultural constants of a slower moving agricultural society. All the confusions, emptinesses, and illusions of our era will then reappear in the poem. But at least the framework of its inception is clear. The space coordinates of myths have been reduced to points on a piece of paper.

The solar origin for a New Years greeting in association with a graphic display of statistical ideas utilized in information theory, illustrate again, how scientific experimentation may color the world of poetry.

"1967 Card" could be developed into a series of compositions with or without holiday timing. The graphic matrix of poetry is present in either case. An elimination of the calendric specification of a holiday will render the time dimension of this kind of poetry more abstract and less comprehensible to more people.

Notes on a Phonetic-Linguistic approach to Prosody

The term prosody here, means all considerations of a writer for the writing of rhythms of speech into poems and songs. It is not my intention to present prosody as a set of simple formulae that pedagogues can teach to poets and songwriters to operate with little effort and less understanding. It is misleading to present the rhythms of speech in songs and poems as mechanical formulae of "feet" and "meters." Rhythms of English are produced by more than a score of variables. Only the capacity of computers can automatically integrate an array of this magnitude. Yet, the minds of writers can handle these variables as separate entities and combine them for special purposes. Here the task is to isolate the variables, clarify their operations, and make them more available to the poet. The first task is a qualitative analysis.

Throughout this discussion references to certain units of language will continuously appear. They are: the phonemes (see p. 5); subphonemic traits (see p. 6, 7); syllables, words, sense groups of three to five successive words that convey meaning; and grammatical categories or the identificational and instructural functions of classes of words (noun, verb, etc.) and considerational rules for sequential order and dependency that concatinate the ordinal properties of grammatic categories into the structure of English.

Our first interest is to clarify the operations of prominence in prosody. "Prominence" means any *perceived conspicuousness* of any language unit that violates the routine stress patterns of a language to convey unusually large amounts of information. This concept includes events outside of linguistic symbols that every language is designed to identify for the listener with a set of instructions. The position taken is that prominence can not be understood without a semantic context—and, in poetry, an aesthetic context . . . all the grammarians not withstanding. We shall now discuss several of the variables that generate "prominence."

Any infrequency in sequential order of language units is likely to produce "prominence." Kaytsingrahnoom with [ts] presents a phoneme sequence that seldom occurs in English. Its appearance in one of the refrains in "Towards Lyra and the Swan" contributes phonemic and syllabic prominence to that refrain. When Robert Frost wrote, *"Something* there *is* that doesn't love a wall," instead of, "There is something that doesn't love a wall, he gave to "something" a positional prominence. Therefor "something" receives more than its normal stress. The meaning is modified. An infrequent sequential order that achieves conspicuousness in syllabic and phonemic and subphonemic units is the "who—we," "who—he," who—she" refrain in "Lyric for a Flute." These examples show that several language units may simultaneously contribute to prominence.

"Prominence is a function of any unusual concentration of language units. This condition for conspicuousness evaluates concentration by the number of occurrences of a language unit per period of time. The period of time may vary between the duration of four to five successive syllables in "a sense group" i.e. 1.25 sec., through the duration of a sentence, a paragraph, or a whole poem. We may also use the *average number of occurrences* of a language unit spoken or written in a representative sample of language. This statistic was utilized in analyzing the tonal energy incorporated in "The Dirge of the Cold." After cursory inspection a sensitive reader will see that "Voices in the Violins," "Lyric for a Flute," "Wood Winds," "Crows," "Inside the Snow," are dominated by different concentrations of phonemes in different populations of words that convey distinctly different acoustic patterns. The nature of these patterns is not obvious because they are constructed with subphonemic features. Examples of some of these features appear on page 5 of the introduction. These phonetic traits are conveyed by the different phonemes of each language. They cannot be written without writing the phonemes that carry them. How then is concentration of a phonetic feature to be achieved? Suppose we wish to concentrate on explosiveness. These are six plosives: [t], [p], [k], unvoiced and [d], [b], [g], voiced. The poet would select or invent syllables and words that contain these sounds and he would crowd his lines with words designed to cue the reader to

express explosiveness throughout his composition. Suppose the poet's interest is explosiveness followed by an uplift, a rise. Then he would follow his plosives with [*l*], because of the uplift in the tongue articulation of [*l*], [t*l*], [p*l*], [k*l*], [d*l*], [b*l*], [g*l*], would begin the sound patterns of a selected set of words or syllables designed to satisfy all the semantic and aesthetic requirements of the poet's theme. The technique is to write an acoustic pattern with a greater frequency than its normal frequency of occurrence. This is where concentration is crucial. Without extra concentration the auditory design of the poetry will not be perceived by the reader. The distinctive acoustic features of all the consonants and vowels in any one language that can be made prominent by concentration are numerous. Features are: glottal roughness, nasal humming, explosiveness, bony-hardness, lippy-softness, bubbly hissing, breathyness along with dark and light, low and high qualities of vowels. They are about 12 in number. When we calculate their combinative potential as 12, or almost half a million acoustic patterns, it becomes evident that the phonetic palette for poetry is a rich one. Its potential has been barely scratched by the prosodic techniques taught today. To explore this potential the art of acoustic prominence based on concentrations of phonetic traits is one of several disciplines available to the poet. This requires understanding of phonetics and linguistics. A treatment of this approach appears in "The Orchestra of the Language," 1959, E. Robson, p. 29-40.

Prominence in prosody may result from identification of an unusual happening that is non-linguistic, i.e. non-verbal. Here we deal with the infrequent occurrences in reality that challenge attention and cause the speaker to articulate with utmost care. When unusual happenings are also emotionally charged their images become even more conspicuous. It is understood that prominence of this type need not be loud. A suddenly whispered statement will stand out with conspicuousness. The juxtaposition of cues for whispering and the loudest cued form of "Sepwidgittinknul" illustrates this kind of prominence in the poem of that title. Images of phrase length are language units most likely to convey this kind of prominence. When the Chinese poet first identified women's eyes with "autumn waves" this prominence occurred. "A sword of a nova," "Dog bit a boy," "Scarlet tears," "Psalm whistling vaginas," "a mink in a crystal cave," evoke unexpected happenings with conspicuous images. Juxtaposition of unexpected images has been the stock in trade of surrealist painters and poets for decades.

Any unusual rhythm or curve of speech energy will contribute to "prominence." A linguistic approach to prosody is essential for establishing the rare or infrequent curves of phonetic power. Less obvious than the shapes of prosodyneic script were the intrinsic power, amplitude and duration rhythms in "Stony River." Many of these rhythms were structured with a rise → fall → rise pattern to express the waviness of water. The energy units that carried these dimensions of intrinsic phonetic power are published in Harvey Fletcher's book "Speech and Hearing," New York, 1958, pages 66-68, and are discussed in "The Orchestra of the Language" 1969, A. S. Barnes and Co., Cranbury,

N. J. The units that conveyed these curves throughout "Stony River" were syllables. It should be observed that the energy levels of intrinsic amplitude, time, and frequency are only averages and even in concerted action do not create more than 3½ levels of stress. Their advantage is the elimination of a need to alter print or introduce artificial cues. These rhythms lack the power and sharpness of prosodynic contours; nor is their performance as reliable without prosodynic cues.

Any unusual or unconventional use of a linguistic unit is likely to generate prominence. This may mean using a noun as a verb, an article or pronoun as a noun, or any other drastic difference in function of a grammatical category. In "Wood Winds" the use of prosodynic stress to reverse grammatical usage was discussed on page 9 of the introduction. Another example is the treatment of auxiliary verbs as nouns in "Pathways of the Suns," in order to associate a sense of timelessness with the potential of the Cosmos. The use of truncated syllables or "phemes" as expressions of feeling in "Quarks" exemplifies an invented unit of prominence.

Any written instruction for readers to speak in a conspicuous acoustic manner is a specification and an expression of intent for prominence. Prosodynes carry such instructions. Cues that link whispering with loudness were mentioned, (see p. 11). A passage dense with high-pitch cues that simultaneously instruct the reader to speak every syllable with the shortest possible time duration terminates the poem, "Voices in the Violins." The vocabulary in this passage is crowded with words that contain "front" vowels with "high" overtones. Without prosodynic cues for high fundamental pitch these lines would be spoken with high overtones. Yet the prosodynes delineate and fix the pitch levels of this passage with a graphic finality that standard English orthography cannot achieve. The author's intent for this passage to be spoken rapidly could not be written with standard English print. Only prosodynes could do this job. Without prosodynes the slow, quiet, middle section of "Voices in the Violins" could not have been clearly written; the loud lines in "Inside the Snow" would not have had their contrastive value shown without prosodynic script. The high information of the pronoun "they" in "Hymn to a Rat Race" could not have been written without prosodynes; nor could the dying-down tonal refrain in "Towards Lyra and the Swan" been written without cues for varying levels of speech. It must be obvious that in poetry many of the infrequently occurring messages of acoustic prominence cannot be written without prosodynes to display the routine stress patterns of a language. A writer cannot continuously instruct his readers to speak specified durations, pauses, power, and pitch levels throughout his script without managing the routine rhythms of his language as well as the infrequent patterns of its prominence. Necessarily, accents of redundancy and information will both be present.

We shall now deal with the more fixed and regular stress patterns of English. The routine accent patterns may be called accents of redundancy. They are the "natural" stress patterns of a language which native speakers use without thinking about them. These are the old codifications of stress.

There are three sources of regularity that generate the predictable stress structures of English. First, the accents of English phonemes which are physiologically predetermined. Secondly, the habit fixed stress patterns of English polysyllablic words. Thirdly, those unrandom tendencies in the distributions of prosodynes. Linguists would call these unrandom tendencies the more constant contours of supra-segmental English, or in a narrow sense "forms of intonation."

The 41 phonemes of English supply the matrix for those patterns of stress that are formed by independent dimensions and qualities of phonemes. These qualities and dimensions were sketchily identified (p. 5-6). A more thorough statement appears in the book "The Orchestra of the Language." More technical data on these constant properties of phonemes are published in Romaine Jacobsen's papers on "distinctive features," in George A. Miller's "Language and Communication" and Harvey Fletcher's "Speech and Hearing." Here we present only one constant influence of phonemes on stress: syllables or words of 4, 5, or 6 phonemes will more likely be stressed than those containing 1, 2, or 3 phonemes. One only needs to listen to a speaking of [a], then [an], then [tan], then [Stan], then [Stand], then [Stands] to perceive that a longer time duration was required to pronounce [Stand] or [Stands], than [a] or [an]. Since time duration is an acoustic dimension of stress we witness here a recurrent and mechanical input to stress as a function of the number of sounds.

The average duration and power (amplitude) of English phonemes is tiny in rapid, weak, little words such as the [a], [an], [it], [he], [to], [she], [in], [net], [pit], [of], [etc.] and syllables as [y], [i], [en], [ic], [le], [an], [an]. These weaker, faster duration phonemes are vowels: [I] in "it," [U] in "wood," [E] in "red," and the trace [a] in "alone." When they combine with rapid consonants [t], [p], [k], [w], and initial [n], [l], they produce acoustically weak units of speech. These weaklings frequently form redundant articles, pronouns, prepositions, and conjunctions. This overlap of low phonetic power in highly redundant words and syllables gives English prosody a wider range of power and duration than French, Spanish, or German phrases. Walt Whitman's rhythms depend on proceeding high information words with weak words "as I lay," "in a dream," etc. Pierre Delattre's papers show quantitatively, the wide range of stress in English phrases.

There are tendencies, but only tendencies and not invariant rules, for some prosodynic curves of English to be constant. I refer to the tendency of a fall-off of power and a drop-down of pitch at the end of English sentences. These trail-offs are frequently accompanied by longer durations. Details on this trend are treated in P. Lieberman's analysis of the breath cycle in his book, "Intonation, Perception and Language," 1967, MIT Press. Violations of this trend by writing high pitched, short duration prosodynes in the last syllable of a line of poetry appear in "Transwhichics 1" and "Transwhichics 2," "Pathways of the Suns," "Tin Rain," etc. These are not high power prominences.

Their effect is moderate because English intonation curves are not constant. Another intonation contour that occurs frequently enough to be noticeable is the rise in pitch of interrogation. Here, too, English is by no means consistent and no rigid rule should be imposed on a tendency. This is said in contradiction to those pedagogues whose obsession for "rules" quashes the poetic potential in the free sounds of English.

Tomes have been written to explain the historical and syntactic genesis of stress on syllables in the polysyllabic lexicon of English. None have told the complete story. Part of the difficulty is that English is a melting pot vocabulary of words from every language. In French polysyllabic words the accent *always* falls on the last syllable; in the three dialects of Yugoslavia the last syllable is *rarely* accented. In English polysyllabic words the accent may fall on *any syllable*.

Our studies show there are factors such as the tendency of noun-like syllables to be stressed in preference to preposition-like prefixes as in deLIGHT, anNOUNCEment, eLIPSE, etc. Low information suffixes [*ion*], [*ent*], [*ence*], in NAtion, CURrent, ESsence, tend to receive weak stress. Clearly, it is the relative importance to the speaker of *what he identifies* that determines stress distribution in English. EXwife, EXconvict, put major stress on the prefixes, not the nouns, because the meaning is enhanced by featuring the statement *former* wife, *former* convict. We see the major semantic determinant again in DEsignation, EXponent, BLUEbird, DISarm, OUT do. In English the

basic factors in stress distribution throughout polysyllabic words are: *the need to identify* and the *subjective intent* of the speaker or writer. Where infrequency of occurrence is great the need to identify becomes the goal of the speaker.

This too brief and unthorough an analysis of routine stress patterns in English requires one last observation: the role of context is cumulative in its information and extends the importance of identification as a major component of stress. That is why grammar appears as a somewhat secondary factor in determining distributions of stress and prominence in English. The information of identification that context contributes is the reason why prosodynic clarification of the writer's intentions are most powerful in the non-contextual English of short poems.

The most important instruction from prosody of the poet is the instruction to enjoy the acoustic patterns of speech as music and to relish the visual imagery evoked by the allusions, associations, and innuendos of language. Every time the poet arranges his script in poetic form he cues the reader to prepare himself for aesthetic pleasure in poetry. The song writers lyric form brings a similar cue to the singer. Aesthetic instructions often conflict and clash with routinized operations and structures of language. The poet strives for fresh and exciting and original prominences, acoustically and visually. He seeks new contexts, new grammars, new image-associations of words and new phonetic patterns.

It is quite unnecessary to bury the creativity of a great art under tomes of linguistic routines, crude formulae, and debatable rules. The poet has an acoustic palette of 12 conspicuous subphonemic features and another set of 8 acoustic dimensions of phonemes. He may also use a set of 46 combinations of prosodyne levels for each syllable that increases the pattern potential as an exponential function of the number of successive syllables up to 46^5. Surely this sound image potential is enormous. How much information this array may carry we don't know. We do know that prosody based on supposed "feet" such as iambuses, anapests, dactyls, etc. will not yield the prosodic information carried by subphonemic features, acoustic dimensions of phonemes, and prosodyne levels. This need not be surprising. Over fifty years ago the experimental psychologist E. W. Scripture, called the "feet" and "meters" taught, authoritatively, as the prosody of English poetry: "a fantastic fabric of fancy without the faintest foundation in fact."